About this Book

The Kentucky Derby is a yearly passion that never ends. Its history captivates the imagination, fascinates the thoughts and tests ones hopes. Few realize it's magic, how it intrigues the mind, or raises so much interest in joining the pursuit. The motivation to attend is baffling. It forces us to reach an unlikely reason that still persists. It might be the mystery of competition that triggers the rhythm for glory.

Bush argues that such an engaging spirit causes the desire and sets the head to spin, the heart to dance and the fascination to peak. Nowhere else is the spark of excitement so apparent than in Kentucky with the emerging of spring. Fans witness the training, follow the flow and endorse their choice. The jockeys ride under the guidance of the trainer and the wiliness of the horse. The horses engage competitively in racing to victory. All such history makes us wonder why the quest. The answer is simple. It's the horse, you fool, nothing but the horse.

DEDICATIONS

TO THE THOROUGHBRED FOAL WHOSE RACING HISTORY CREATES A RECORD THAT EXCITES AND PLEASES SO MANY FANS.

TO THE FANS WHOSE ATTENDANCE HAS EVOLVED WITH THE AGING OF THIS REMARKABLE EVENT, THE KENTUCKY DERBY.

TO THE OWNERS, TRAINERS AND JOCKEYS WHOSE ENGAGING KNOW-HOW AND SUPPORT BINDS IT ALL TOGETHER.

CHAPTERS

INTRODUCTION

1. Kentucky Derby: How It Started………………………1
2. Admission – Seating Arrangement……………… 15
3. Sites on the Ground……………………………………19
4. Track Services and Facilities……………………26
5. Locating Food and Drink…………………………..27
6. Daily Racing Programs, Tip Sheets………………30
7. Factors Affecting Wins…………………………….34
8. Famous Owners………………………………………50
9. Identifying Leading Trainers……………………59
10. Winning and Other Talented Jockeys……………..67
11. How to Interpret Racing Statistics………………75
12. Race Horse Selections………………………………83
13. Wagering – Types of Bets………………………..87
14. You Be the Judge……………………………………96
15. Travel Arrangements to the Track……………..106
16. Arrival – Parking………………………………….109
17. Places to Stay………………………………………111

INTRODUCTION

This guide focuses on improving the racing fan's knowledge of the Kentucky Derby. It shows ways to manage their activities while attending this spectacular event. It should enhance their understanding of selecting and betting on winning horses.

The history of the famous Kentucky Derby is discussed in Chapter 1. This race began in 1875 at a Louisville race track that became known as Churchill Downs in 1883. The founders, Meriwether Clark Jr and his father Meriwether Clark Sr planned the development of Churchill Downs. They obtained funds by selling shares in the planned development and by leasing the site location from their relatives John and Henry Churchill to construct the track.

Chapter 2 provides racing fans some Important details concerned with arrival to the track and on-going changes that occur in parking before and during race week.

Instructions are described for purchasing tickets. Directions about seating arrangements are covered prior to the race and on race day in Chapter 3

To improve the fan's on-track activities, specific areas on the grounds including betting sites, restrooms and health facilities are identified in Chapter 4.

Chapter 5 describes some of the various sources for obtaining different kinds of food and drinks.

Information about ways to obtain and interpret racing of the horses entered in the Kentucky Derby are covered in Chapter 6.

Numerous factors are listed and evaluated in their importance as affecting the outcome of the race in Chapter 7.

Chapter 8 identifies some the previous winning owners and the strategies required to win the Kentucky Derby.

Famous trainers and their racing accomplishments are recognized in Chapter 9 as a means to increase the racing fan's opportunities for selecting a trainer capable of training a winning horse.

Chapter 10 lists the most successful winning jockeys and describes how their riding talents have led to winning horses.

Statistical information in Chapter 12 is presented for racing fans that might be used to Improve their understanding of performance of current Derby starters.

The choice of a winning horse is made easier by reading and evaluating the racing data available in Chapter 13.

Details are offered about how to bet, as well as information about the types of bets in Chapter 14

Several racing scribes have identified some past horses they have chosen as the most outstanding winners of the Kentucky Derby. While these selections add to fan excitement of the event, an argument can be made that races having tight closing outcomes have produced more thrilling everlasting enjoyment for fans. Chapter 15 points out several examples of these exciting outcomes.

In Chapter 16, travel arrangements are provided to help fans locate Churchill Downs. Directions and maps are provided making it easier for fans to reach the track.

Places to stay nearby the track are listed according to proximity of the track in Chapter 17.

CHAPTER 1

KENTUCKY DERBY: HOW IT STARTED

The Kentucky Derby has been recognized as the greatest two minutes in sports. It is one of the highest-attended sporting events in the world. At least 160,000 horse racing fans per year have attended the event over the past 10 years. It has been run continuously every year since 1875, marking 2019 as the 145th running.[1,2]

The Kentucky Derby is held on the First Saturday of May.

It began with the founding of the New Louisville Jockey Club (Churchill Downs) in 1872.[3] Meriwether Lewis Clark Jr, a 26-year-old entrepreneur of Louisville, Kentucky, ventured to Surry, England and France in 1872. While attending the horse races at North Down, Epsom Race Course, he saw the running of the Epsom Derby. Intrigued by the spectacular event, he envisioned that a similar happening might be conducted and showcased in Louisville, Kentucky.

Meriwether Clark Jr had important family connections on both sides of the family.[4] His grandfather was the famous explorer William Clark of the Lewis and Clark Expedition. His father. Meriwether Lewis Clark, Sr., born in St. Louis, Missouri, became a leading architect and civil engineer and served in the Mexican War and the Black Hawk War. While on duty in the Black Hawk War, he traveled to Louisville, Kentucky. Clark Jr met and married Abigail Prather Churchill in 1834. The couple had seven children. Abigail belonged to the prominent Churchill family that had moved to Kentucky in 1787. She died in 1852.

Clark Sr resigned from service after the Black Hawk War. However, encouraged to re-enlist during the Civil War, he served as a Colonel in the Confederate Armed Forces. On assignment to Richmond, Virginia, he served in the Ordnance Division for a limited time. Later, he directed Virginia's Reserve Forces in General Robert E. Lee's Unit in the Northern Virginia Campaign. Reassigned during the Appomattox Campaign, he was imprisoned following the Battle of Sayler's Creek, near Amelia Court House, on April 5, 1865. After release from Union Forces, he returned to Louisville and married Jula Davidson. He served as Commander of Cadets at Kentucky Military Institute located nearby Louisville.

Clark Jr returned from Europe in 1872 in pursuit of his vision of having a Kentucky Derby in Louisville. An incredible combination of factors made the challenge of doing so likely. He had an exceptional opportunity via a powerful fan base as many Kentuckians knew about thoroughbred racing and loved the sport. He needed thoroughbreds to race and horse owners/horse breeders in surrounding counties, such as Shelby, Fayette and Bourbon and those of northern Kentucky namely Boone, Kenton and Campbell near Cincinnati to improve his chances. His uncles were Henry Churchill and John Churchill.[5]

The Churchill brothers were grandsons of Armistead Churchill Jr and Elizabeth Bakewell of Middlesex, Virginia. Samuel Churchill came across Cumberland Gap into Kentucky with his parents at age six. The Churchill family settled near Louisville and had purchased a 300-acre tract of land in southern Jefferson County. Samuel became a farmer, landowner and a member of the Kentucky Legislature both in the Senate and the House. Samuel owned a home called Spring Grove that was built on the property before 1804. He lived on the property located north of Preston Street Road and south of Eastern Parkway. Later, he willed the property to his brothers Henry and John. Part of the property became the site of Churchill Downs.

Clark Jr leased 80 acres of the Churchill property from uncles Henry and John. Both uncles had recognized social positions and provided some financial and family support. Henry was Justice of Peace in 1793 and became an Assistant to Stephen Ormsby the Circuit Court Judge of Jefferson County in 1803. He served as one the Trustees of the Jefferson Seminary in 1798 that was granted 6,000 acres by the Legislature.

The leased property was located within approximately four miles from the city's center. As founder of the Louisville Jockey Club, Clark Jr had made several friends and had acquired considerable expertise dealing with rules and regulations of thoroughbred racing. Still, he lacked additional monies needed for construction of the track, stables and grandstand. He invited others to invest in the venture and built a solid base to begin. He sold 320 memberships at $100 each. Clark Sr, a prominent engineer, contributed his architectural skills by designing certain of the structures and facilities needed. Once these plans had been completed, the initial thoroughbred racing of the Kentucky Derby, the Kentucky Oaks, and the Clark Handicap occurred on May 17, 1875. The racetrack named after the Churchill Family became known as Churchill Downs and the official landmark site for the Kentucky Derby in 1883. The track has been considered as "America's Most Historic Racetrack."[6]

TIMELINE (Selected Findings)

1875: First race designated as the Kentucky Derby held on May 17 opening at the Louisville race course.

1883: Newly constructed racetrack given name of Churchill Downs.

1895: Members of the New Louisville Jockey Club advanced the plans leading to the construction of two Twin Spires above the grandstand at a cost of $100,000.

1928: Churchill Downs Incorporated recognized as publicly held stock on NASDAQ stock exchange.

1937: Churchill Downs became incorporated as a racetrack.

1938: Churchill Downs formed a committee to operate the racetrack as a non-profit entity and made annual donations of $1.5 million to charity over a 10-year period.

1952-55: New barns, sprinkler systems and improved seating arrangements were completed.

1959-1966: Additional improvements were made in seating and construction of the museum started

1982: The pari-mutuel racing system was computerized and construction of the $7 million Kentucky Derby Museum completed.

1984: Construction began with $25 million renovations of the Paddock, Clubhouse, barns and the turf course.

2002-2003: Renovations followed with the building of 60 luxury suites, installation of more seating, a new entrance and expansion of the Turf Club.

2005: $150 million spent on completion of grandstand and clubhouse.

2009-2010: Night racing began initially following $4 million placement of lights and improved facilities made around the track. Approximately 27,000 fans attended.

2012: Construction of the 6th floor "The Mansion" at a cost of $9 million that accommodates approximately 320 fans.

2018: $70 million upgrades to the Starting Gate Suites, addition of Paddock and Clubhouse Gates, 50 acres of parking spaces, and a bus depot.

    The Kentucky Derby is often called the "Run for the Roses." The red rose has been the official flower of the race since 1904. The winner's garland draped on the horse shoulders features more than 400 roses.

    Jody Demling in the May 2, 2018, edition of SportsLine, described that: "The annual Grade I Stakes race, the 'Run for the Roses,' has long been the biggest showcase of American horse racing." Quite a meaningful remark from a racing analyst who has predicted the winner of the Kentucky Derby for 10 straight years.

In a highly favorable comment, Cindy Pierson Dulay, ThoughtCo April 7, 2018, described "The **Kentucky Derby** is inarguably the most famous and important race in North America for 3-year-old thoroughbreds. It's a hands down favorite among racing fans and some of the races have been much more memorable than others."[2]

KENTUCKY DERBY WINNERS[8]

YEAR	WINNER	TRAINER	JOCKEY	OWNER
2018	Justify	Bob Baffert	Mike Smith	China Horse Club, WinStar Farm (2:04.2 sloppy)
2017	Always Dreaming	Todd Pletcher	John R Velazquez	Bklyn Boyz Stables (2:03.59 wet fast)
2016	Nyquist	Doug O'Neill	Mario Gutierrez	Reddam Racing (2;01.31 fast)
2015	American Pharoah	Bob Baffert	Victor Espinosa	Ahmed Zakat
2014	California Chrome	Art Sherman	Victor Espinosa	Steve & Carolyn Coburn; Perry & Denise Martin
2013	Orb	Claude R. McGaughey III	Joel Rosario	Stuart Janney III & Phipps Stable (2:02.89 sloppy)
2012	I'll Have Another	Doug O'Neill	Mario Gutierrez	J. Paul Reddam LLC.
2011	Animal Kingdom	H. Graham Motion	John R. Velazquez	Team Valor Intern.
2010	Super Saver	Todd Pletcher	Calvin Borel	Win Star Farm (2:04.45 sloppy)

Year	Horse	Trainer	Jockey	Owner
2009	Mine that Bird	B. Wooley, Jr	Calvin Borel	Double Eagle & Bueno Suerte (2:02.66 sloppy)
2008	Big Brown	Richard Dutrow Jr	Kent J. Desormeaux	IEAH Stable; Paul P. Pompa, Jr (2:01.82 fast)
2007	Street Sense	Carl Nafzger	Calvin Borel	James B. Tafel
2006	Barbaro	Michael Matz	Edgar Prado	Lael Stables
2005	Giacomo	John Shirreffs	Mike Smith	Jerome Moss
2004	Smarty Jones	John Servis	Stewart Elliott	Someday Farm
2003	Funny Cide	Barclay Tagg	Jose Santos	Sackatoga Stable (2:01 19)
2002	War Emblem	Bob Baffert	Victor Espinosa	Thoroughbred CP (2:01 1/3 fast)
2001	Monarchos	John T. Ward	Jorge Chavez	John C. Oxley (1:59 97 fast)
2000	Fusaichi Pegasus	Neil D. Drysdale	Kent J. Desormeaux	Fusao Sekiguchi (2:01 fast)
1999	Charismatic	D. Wayne Lukas	Chris Antley	Robert B & Beverly Lewis
1998	Real Quiet	Bob Baffert	K. J. Desormeaux	Mike Pegram
1997	Silver Charm	Bob Baffert	Gary Stevens	Robert & Beverly Lewis
1996	Grindstone	D. Wayne Lukas	Jerry Bailey	Overbrook Farm (2:01 fast)
1995	Thunder Gulch	D. Wayne Lukas	Gary Stevens	Michael Tabor (2:01 1/5 fast)
1994	Go for Gin	Nick Zito	Chris McCarron	Wm J. Condre & Joseph M. Cornacchia
1993	Sea Hero	MacKenzie	Jerry Bailey	Rokeby Stable

		Miller		
1992	Lil E. Tee	Lynn Whiting	Pat Day	W. Cal Parte
1991	Strike the Gold	Nick Zito	Chris Antley	BCC Stable
1990	Unbridled	Carl Nafzger	Craig Parret	Frances A. Genter
1989	Sunday Silence	Charles Edward	Patrick Valenzuela	H-G-W Partners
1988	Winning Colors	D. Wayne Lukas	Gary Stevens	Eugene V. Klein
1987	Alysheba	Charles Van Berg	Chris McCaron	D & P. Scharbauer
1986	Ferdinand	Charles Edward Whittingham	William Shoemaker	Elizabeck A. Keck
1985	Spend a Buck	Cam Gambolati	Angel Cordera, Jr	Dennis Diaz (2:00 1/5 fast)
1984	Swale	Woodford C. Stephens	Laffit Pincay, Jr	Claiborne Farm
1983	Sunny's Halo	David C. Cross	Eddie Delahoussaye	D. J. Foster Stable
1982	Gato Del Sol	Edwin J Greyson	Eddie Delahoussaye	Hancock & Peters
1981	Pleasant Colony	John P. Campo	Jorge Velasquez	Buckland Farm
1980	Genuine Risk	LeRoy Jolly	Jacinto Vasquez	Diana M. Firestone
1979	Spectacular Bid	Grover Delp	Ronnie Franklin	Hawksworth Farm
1978	Affirmed	Lazaro Barrera	Steve Cauthen	Harbor View Farm (2:01 1/5 fast)
1977	Seattle Slew	Wm. H. Turner	Jean Cruguet	Karen L. Taylor

Year	Horse	Trainer	Jockey	Owner
1976	Bold Forbes	Lazaro Barrera	Angel C. Cordero, Jr	E. Rodriguez Tirol
1975	Foolish Pleasure	LeRoy Jolley	Jacinto Vasquez	John L. Greer
1974	Cannonade	Woodford C. Stephens	Angel C. Cordero, Jr	John M. Olin
1973	Secretariat	Lucien Laurin	Ron Turcotte	Meadow Stable (1:59 2/5 fast)
1972	Riva Ridge	Lucien Laurin	Ron Turcotte	Meadow Stud
1971	Canonero II	Juan Arias	Gustavo Avila	Edgar Caleb
1970	Dust Commander	Don Combs	Mike Manganello	Robert E. Lehmann
1969	Majestic Prince	John Longden	William Hardtack	Frank M. McMahon
1968	Forward Pass	Henry Forrest	Ismael Valenzuela	Calumet Farm (2:00 3/5 fast)
1967	Proud Clarion	Loyd Gentry, Jr	Robert Usury	Darby Dan Farm
1966	Kauai King	Henry Forrest	Don Broomfield	Ford Stable
1965	Lucky Debonair	Frank Catrone	William Shoemaker	Ada L. Rice (2:01 1/5 fast)
1964	Northern Dancer	Horatio Luro	William Hardtack	Windfields Farm (2:00 fast)
1963	Chateaugay	James R. Conway	Braulio Baeza	Darby Dan Farm
1962	Decidedly	Horatio Luro	William Hardtack	El Peco Ranch (2:00 2/5 fast)
1961	Carry Back	Jack Price	John Sellers	Katherine Price
1960	Venetian Way	Victor J. Sovinski	William Hardtack	Sunny Blue Farm

Year	Horse	Trainer	Jockey	Owner
1959	Tomy Lee	Frank E. Childs	William Shoemaker	Frank & Juliette Turner
1958	Tim Tam	H.A. Jones	Ismael Valenzuela	Calumet Farm
1957	Iron Leige	H.A. Jones	William Hardtack	Calumet Farm
1956	Needles	Hugh Fontaine	David Erb	D & H. Stable
1955	Swaps	M.A. Tenney	William Shoemaker	Rex C. Elsworth
1954	Determine	Wm. Molter	Raymond York	Andrew J. Crevolin
1953	Dark Star	Ed. Hayard	Henry Moreno	Cain Hoy Stable
1952	Hill Gail	Ben A. Jones	Ed. Arcaro	Calumet Farm
1951	Count Turf	Sol Rutchick	Conn McCreary	Jack J. Amiel
1950	Middlegrd.	Max Hirsch	William Boland	King Ranch
1949	Ponder	Ben A. Jones	Steve Brooks	Calumet Farm
1948	Citation	Ben A. Jones	Ed. Arcaro	Calumet Farm
1947	Jet Pilot	Tom Smith	Eric Guerin	Main Chance Farm
1946	Assault	Max Hirsch	Warren Methinks	King Ranch
1945	Hoop, Jr	Ivan H. Parke	Ed. Arcaro	Fred W. Hooper
1944	Pensive	Ben A. Jones	Conn McCreary	Calumet Farm
1943	Count Fleet	G.D. Cameron	John Longden	Fannie Hertz
1942	Shut Out	John Gaver Sr	Wayne D. Wright	Greentree Stable

Year	Horse	Trainer	Jockey	Owner
1941	Whirlaway	Ben A. Jones	Ed. Arcaro	Calumet Farm (2:01 2/5 fast)
1940	Gallahadion	Roy Waldron	Carroll Bierman	Milky Way Farm
1939	Johnstown	James Stout	James Fitzsimmons	Belair Stud
1938	Lawrin	Ben A. Jones	Ed. Arcaro	Herbert M. Woolf
1937	War Admiral	George Conway	Charlie Kurtsinger	Glen Riddle Farm
1936	Bold Venture	Max Hirsch	Ira Hanford	Morton L. Schwartz
1935	Omaha	James Fitzsimmons	William Sanders	Belair Stud
1934	Cavalcade	Robert A. Smith	Mack Garner	Brookmeade
1933	Broker's Tip	Herbert John Thompson	Don Meade	Edward R. Bradley
1932	Burgoo King	Herbert John Thompson	Basil James	Edward R. Bradley
1931	Twenty Grand	James Rowe, Jr	Charlie Kurtsinger	Greentree Stable
1930	Gallant Fox	James Fitzsimmons	Earl Sande	Blair Stud
1929	Clyde Van Dusen	Clyde Van Dusen	Linus McAtee	H. P. Gardner
1928	Reigh Count	Bert Mitchell	Charlie Long	Fannie Hertz
1927	Whiskery	Fred Hopkins	Linus McAtee	Henry P. Whitney
1926	Bubbling Over	Herbert John Thompson	Albert Johnson	Edward R. Bradley
1925	Flying Ebony	William Duke	Earle Sande	Gifford A. Cochran

Year	Horse	Trainer	Jockey	Owner
1924	Black Gold	Hanly Webb	John D. Mooney	Rosa M. Hoots
1923	Zev	D.J Leary	Earle Sande	Rancocas Stable
1922	Morvich	Fred Burfew	Albert Johnson	Benjamin Block
1921	Behave Yourself	Herbert John Thompson	Charles Thompson	Edward R. Bradley
1920	Paul Jones	William Garth	Ted Rice	Rai Parr
1919	Sir Barton	H. Guy Bedwell	Wm. Garth	J. K. L. Ross
1918	Exterminator	Henry McDaniel	William Knapp	Willis Sharpe Kilmer
1917	Omar Khayam	C.T. Patterson	Charles Borel	C. K. G. Billings & Frederick Johnson
1916	George Smith	Hollie Hughes	John Loftus	John Sanford
1915	Regret	James Rowe Sr	Joe Notter	Henry P. Whitney
1914	Old Rosebud	Frank Weir	John McCabe	H. C. Applegate
1913	Donerail	Thomas P. Hayes	Roscoe Goose	Thomas P. Hayes
1912	Worth	Frank M. Taylor	Carol Hugh Hallenbeck	Henry C. Shilling
1911	Meridian	Albert Ewing	George Archibald	Richard F. Carman
1910	Donau	George Ham	Robert Herbert	William Gerst
1909	Wintergreen	Vincent Powers	Charles Mack	Jerome B. Respell
1908	Stone Street	J. W. Hall	Arthur Pickens	C. E. & J. Hamilton
1907	Pink Star	W. H. Fizer	Andy Minder	J. Hal Woodford

Year	Winner	Trainer	Jockey	Owner
1906	Sir Huon	Pete Coyne	Roscoe Troller	Bashford Manor
1905	Agile	Robert Tucker	Jack Martin	Samuel S. Brown
1904	Elwood	Charlie E. Durnell	Frank Prior	Mrs. C. E. Darnell
1903	Judge *Himes*	John P Mayberry	Harold Booker	Charles Ellison
1902	Alan-a-Dale	Thomas Clay	Jimmy Winkfield	T. C. McDowell
1901	His Eminence	Frank B. Van Meter	Jimmy Winkfield	Frank B. Van Meter
1900	Lieut. Gibson	Charles Hughes	Jimmy Boland	Charles H. Smith
1889	Manuel	Robert Walden	Fred Tarai	A. H. & D. H. Morris
1898	Plaudit	John E. Madden	Willie Simms	John E. Madden
1887	Typhoon II	J. C. Cahn	Buttons	J. C. Cahn
1896	Ben Brush	Hardy Campbell Jr	Willie Simms	Mike F. Dwyer
1895	Halma	Byron McClelland	Soup Perkins	Byron McClelland
1894	Chant	H. Eugene Leigh	Frank Goodale	H. Eugene Leigh & R. Rose
1893	Lookout	William McDaniel	Eddie Kunze	Cushing & Orth
1892	Azra	John H. Morris	Alonzo Clayton	Bashford Manor Stg.
1891	Kingman	Dud Allen	Isaac Murphy	Jacobin Stable
1890	Riley	Edward Corrigan	Isaac Murphy	Edward Corrigan
1889	Spokane	John Rodegap	Tom Riley	Noah Armstrong
1888	Macbeth II	John Campbell	George Covington	Chicago Stable

Year	Horse	Jockey	Trainer	Owner
1887	Montrose	John McGinty	Isaac Lewis	Labold Brothers
1886	Ben Ali	Jim Murphy	Paul Duffy	J.B.A. Hangin
1885	Joe Cotton	Abe Petty	Erskine Henderson	James T. Williams
1884	*Buchanan*	William Byrd	Isaac Murphy	William Cottrill, Samuel Brown
1883	<u>Leonatus</u>	Raleigh Colton	William Donohue	Chinn & Morgan
1882	Apollo	Green B. Morris	Babe Hurd	Morris & Patton
1881	Hindoo	Hames G Rowe Sr	James McLaughlin	Dwyer Bros. Stable
1880	Fonso	Tice Hutsell	George Garret Lewis	J. Snell Shawn
1879	Lord Murphy	George Rice	Charlie Shaker	Darden & Co
1878	Day Star	Lee Paul	Jimmy Carter	T. J. Nichols
1887	Baden-Baden	Edward D. Brown	William Walker	Daniel Swigger
1876	Vagrant	James Williams	Bob Swim	William Astor Jr
1875	Aristides	Ansel Williamson	Oliver Lewis	Hal. P. McGrath

CHAPTER 2

ADMISSION – SEATING

Main Entrance to Paddock (Gate 1) to Track (right) and Kentucky Derby Museum (left): Barbaro Statue in Front Entrance. (MMB)

Kentucky Derby Museum Entrance (MMB)

The Kentucky Derby Museum is an interesting place to visit. Exhibits of various types of Derby articles are on display. Racing trophies, awards, artwork, photographs and racing colors can excite the watchful eye. One can learn about Birth and Stages in the life of the thoroughbred. Examples of thoroughbred Bloodlines are especially intriguing.

Library books and movies featuring stories about some of the famous Derby thoroughbreds, the jockeys who rode them and the trainers who managed their careers are available. The D. Wayne Lukas Collection of racing memorabilia is particularly interesting. Featured is Churchill Downs First Electric Starting Gate and a display of horseshoes from the Horseshoe Hall of Fame. There is a fascinating collection of Women's Derby Hats.

The Gift Shop keeps a vast assemblage of party items on hand for the happy party-goer on Derby Day. They include tote bags, horseshoes, Derby Cups, magnets and tickets for guided tours of Churchill Downs.

The Derby Cafe is open to the public. No Museum admission fee is needed to eat there.

The Museum offers services suitable for rental space, special events, convention meetings and catering functions.

Buying Tickets[1, 2, 3]

Tickets can be purchased at a pre-sale directly or on-line from Churchill Downs. The secondary market of buying on-line or directly usually raises the cost. There are various types of seating and the prices increase with the degree of hospitality.

- General admission – entrance to the ground level of the main area of the track and infield. Seating is on the ground
- Lower grandstand – 1st floor tier, bleacher seats – no back
- Lower grandstand - 2nd floor tier, bleacher seats – no back
- Grandstand – 3rd tier – tip-up seat with back
- Grandstand terrace – stadium seats with back
- Clubhouse – Section 110 – stadium style with back
- Lower Clubhouse – outside, folding chairs, six per box
- Second Tier Clubhouse – Section 212, box, folding chairs
- Third Tier Clubhouse – six per box, folding chairs
- Court Yard – between Sections 118-119. Next to Winner's Circle and Paddock Walkway – folding chairs

- Millionaires Row – 4th and 6th floors, dining room, table of 8, private viewing platform
- The Mansion – 6th floor, 296 tickets available, personal seat license individually negotiated, private elevator, most expensive
- Angry Orchard Club - A new section at the head of the turf course. Fans can enjoy seeing the horses load at the starting gate.
- Vineyard Vines Club - A modern construction located at the at the first turn (Formerly Section 110).
- Luxury Trackside Club - A new facility located at the homestretch of the turf track.

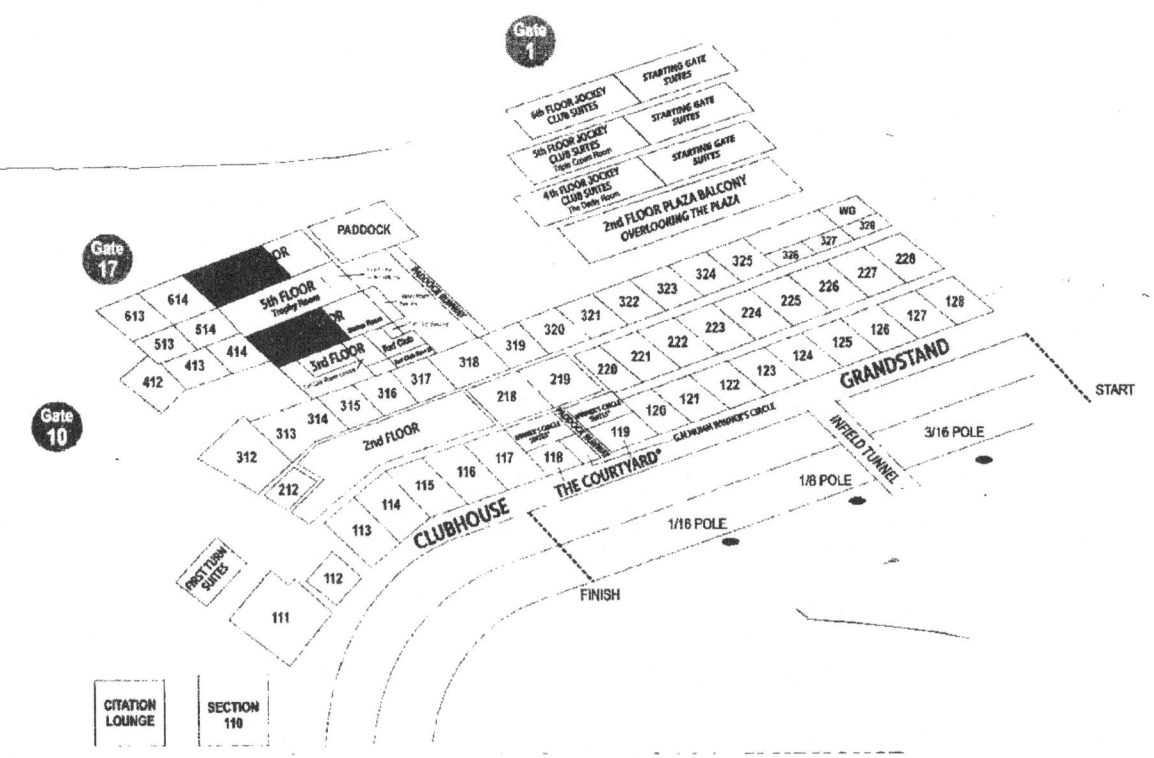

Paddock gates (1 and 17) near Central Avenue. Clubhouse Gate (10) at Longfield Avenue.

CHAPTER 3

SITES ON THE GROUNDS

Churchill Downs covers 115 acres. It has over 1.7 million square feet under roof.[1] Joseph Dominic Baldez a noted Louisville architect, designed the magnificent Twin Spires located above the Grandstand in 1884 that the public first saw at the 11th Kentucky Derby.[2] The octagonal Twin Spires characterizes the Kentucky Derby and is the registered trademark of Churchill Downs.

View of Paddock After Front Gate Entrance. Note Stalls in Rear. (MMB)

View of the Race Screen Tote Board Over the Paddock Building (MMB). Fans Can See Numerous Details of Value Prior to, During and After Each Race.

View of Grandstand and Clubhouse at the Clubhouse Turn and Finish Line (RS). The first Grandstand had a seating capacity of 4,500 with a standing aisle capacity of 1,500. Built in 1894 and 250 feet long, it consisted of red brick. Note the lights above the present Grandstand and Clubhouse added for night racing.

The dirt track at Churchill Downs is a mile long. Horses enter the starting gate in a chute. They race one half mile, race around a turn ending at the head of the stretch and then move toward the finish line in front of the Grandstand.

For the Kentucky Derby, the horse's start at the 1/4 - mile marker in front of the Grandstand, race forward passing the Clubhouse and circle the clubhouse turn, and then continue along the backside. They race around the far turn, reach the 1/4 - mile marker near the head of the stretch and race to the finish line.

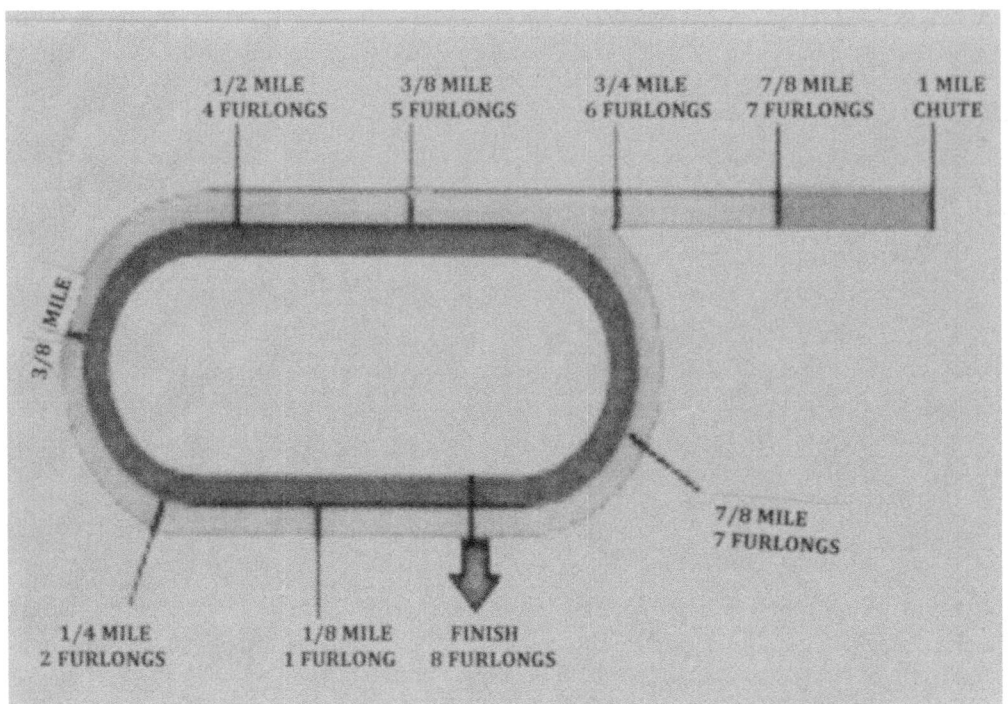

**Churchill Downs Oval – 1 Mile with Furlong Markers
Derby Starting Gate at 1/4 Mile Marker at Head of Stretch:
Horses Race Around Two Turns in the Kentucky Derby**

Infield Structures

The Infield Tunnel opens near 1/4 Mile Marker. The opening on the other side of the track is behind the Kentucky Derby Museum and Gift Shop. The Derby Café and a fountain are nearby. The tunnel passes under the track and opens next to the Turf Suites in the infield.

Several buildings in the Infield offer enjoyment for fans.

Infield Club

Winner's Circle

Tote Board

Starting Gate Turf Suite – Near 1/4 Mile Pole

8th Marker Turf Suite – Near 1/8 Mile Pole

16th Turf Suite – Near I/16 Mile Pole

Finish Line Turf Suite – Near Finish Line Pole

Video Screen – Largest 4 K LED Board in the World, built by Panasonic it covers 16,000 square feet

The Winner's Circle allows fans to see the owners, trainer, jockey and the winner after the race. The world's largest Video Screen permits fans to watch the Kentucky Derby and other races. Four luxury Turf Suites, each with private seating up to 85 fans, can be rented. Located at ground level to the track, fans can see the horses pass at close range.

The Infield Club has a well-supplied bar and a video lounge creating a sports/bar arrangement. Outdoor hospitality is provided for fans wagering at betting windows or self-service machines. Other facilities including restrooms are available.

Older Display of the Viewing Stand Located in the Infield Near the Finish Line Offers the Fans an Opportunity to View Winning Horses of the Ky Derby. (Library Of Congress)

Aerial View of Horse Boarding Stable Located on the Backside Along Longfield Avenue (lower left) – A Total of 1,400 Stalls Are Available. Tours Can Be Arranged for Fans and American and Spanish Style Foods Can Be Obtained at the Track Kitchen.

Older View of the Clubhouse, Grandstand and Track When the Track Was Finished. Note the Twin Spires That Helped Make Churchill Downs Famous. (Library of Congress).

CHAPTER 4

TRACK SERVICES AND FACILITIES

On a busy day such as the Kentucky Derby, the fans need to know the location of a First Aid Station and other suitable accommodations including rest rooms that are available.

Rest Rooms - each of the six floors has segregated rest rooms for men and women.[1]

Floor 1 (Ground) – Gate 10, Skye Terrace, Media Center, Jockey Club, Clubhouse; Sections 115-122

Floor 2 – Sections 315-317, junction 218/318-323, Clubhouse

Floor 3 – Near Gate 10; between Gates 10 and 17; Skye Terrace, Clubhouse, Roses Lounge, Turf Club, across from Finish Line

Floor 4 – Near Gate 17; Skye Terrace, Millionaires Row,; Gate 1 Jockey Club Suites

Floor 5 – Gate 17; Skye Terrace, Clubhouse; Gate 1 – Triple Crown Room, Jockey Club Suites, Sections 501-520

Floor 6 – Gate 17; Skye Terrace, Clubhouse; Gate 1 Jockey Club Suites

Infield – Center of track, near Winner's Circle, Infield Club and Turf Suites

First Aid – Gate 1, Ground floor; near Derby Museum and General Offices

Wheel Chairs – Guests should inquire about the availability of wheelchairs before going to the track. Call 502-636-4450. They should bring their own if they have one. Otherwise, they may have to wait. Assistance is available to and from seating locations. Upon entering the track, go to Guest Services located at any gate and ask for assistance.

Accessible Seating

Floor 1 (Ground)-Sections 115-117, Rows B and D, Section 126, Row 0, use the ramp behind 126; section 128, Rows U and V, use ramp behind 128.

Floor 2. – From the ground floor, take the wheelchair elevator near the Skye Terrace lobby to the second floor. Pass through the double doors to Section 115-seats K02-KO8, K15, K 17, L02-L04; Section 16 – K03, K09. Ramp is available at Sections 115 and 116.

Floor 3 – Reserved Ticket required (502-636-4400) Sections 315 seats C01-13, C15-20; Sections 317 seats C01, C10, C12-23. Lift available in Section 220-320 or take wheelchair elevator from ground floor to the sections.

CHAPTER 5

LOCATING FOOD AND DRINK

Numerous small food and drink sources are available on the grounds.[1,2] Food carts and walkup service counters are plentiful. If you have proper tickets, food and drink can be acquired for the Kentucky Derby and Kentucky Oaks at the following reserved areas:

1. **Court Yard Lounge** – reserved for Kentucky Derby and Kentucky Oaks

2. **Derby Room** – second floor

3. **Aristides Lounge features the Loft Dining Room** – second floor

4. **Roses Lounge** - has the famous Matt Winn Dining Room

5. **Stakes Room**

6. **Millionaire's Row and Skye Terrace** – Overlooks the tracks finish line.

7. **Court Yard at the Downs after Dark** – An outdoor picnic area with seating and dining tables and indoor access to hospitality.

8. **Citation Lounge** - Because of the vast space the Clubhouse covers, the Citation and the Secretariat Lounges are available. The Citation lounge is a classic hospitality venue located behind Section 111. The area is climate-controlled and so difficult weather conditions outside are avoided. There is a complimentary gourmet fare, a cash-basis bar, and self-service wagering machines. TV coverage allows for viewing events occurring outside. You can enter the track from the lounge through Gate 10.

9. **Secretariat Lounge** – The lounge is located on the second

floor near the food court just above Gate 17. It is climate-controlled within, includes complimentary food buffet, a premium open bar, self-service wagering kiosks, and simulcast TV coverage of the surrounding activities.

Most specialty dining rooms feature the Chefs Table Buffet. You might like to drink a "Mint Julep." It is an alcoholic beverage available on Derby and Oaks days. The ingredients are Kentucky Bourbon whisky diluted with a little water poured over crushed or shaved ice and fresh mint leaves.

10. **Starting Gate Rooftop Terrace -** A new area located on the 7th floor of the grandstand. Standard seating is offered and if the fans desire hospitality accommodations this is the place to be.

11. **Track Kitchen –** The track kitchen on the backside is open to individuals holding a Kentucky Horse Racing License. American and Spanish style foods are on hand.

12. **Infield Club –** A sport's bar centered in the Infield is available to fans during the Kentucky Derby and Kentucky Oaks. The Video Lounge, betting windows, and self - service betting machines make it easy for fans to watch and bet on the races.

CHAPTER 6

RACING PROGRAMS, TIP SHEETS, NEWS

Daily racing programs, tip sheets, betting strategies, and pedigree analyses are available at some websites. Some of the information is free, but you may have to pay a fee if you seek professional advice on a subject or seek technical information. Here are the names of some well-known sources:

Daily Racing Form – www.drf.com[1]
Equibase.com[2]
Brisnet.com[3]
Horse Racing Nation.com[4]
Blood Horse.com[5]
TrueNicks.com[6]
US Racing News and Handicapping Reports[7]
Paulick Report. com[8]

Daily Racing Form (DRF) – Registration is required and signup is free. Data on entries with odds, scratches and changes, as well as previous results charts are free on the Internet. Past Performances and other handicapping material are available for a fee, including clocker reports and pedigree data. The Form provides past performances for almost every race in states around the U.S.A. You can buy the Form at any track and at some newsstands. Once you access the website, you can download the Form through the Form Finder.

Equibase - Available on the Internet, there is **easy** access to racing information at most racetracks across the country. Listed are workouts at various distances, daily entries with odds, changes, scratches, and results charts as well as jockey and trainer stats. Past performance information is sold.

Brisnet - Signup is free to access the basic data. The programs of this business focus on ratings systems that permit one to scrutinize details of a horse's performance, as well as pedigree background. Examples include:

BRIS Prime Power Rating - A rating based on analyses of a huge number of race characteristics, namely condition, speed, class, place, form, weight, distance and performance. It can be used to identify key horses expected to win a high percentage of the time. Studies show a horse rating better than 3 points over others in the field wins 39% of the time; one rating 10 points over others wins 55 % of the time.

BRIS Pace Ratings – a number given to a horse's speed at the lst call, 2nd call and late pace.

BRIS Pedigree Ratings - a value that determines the sire's history racing under different track conditions, such as fast, wet, distance and turf.

Such data about past performance provide valuable information to breeders and handicappers.

Horse Racing Nation – A fantastic source of current information and reference material covering Expert Picks, Stakes Analyses, Guaranteed Tip

Sheet, Free Past Performances, TVG Expert Picks, and details concerned with Kentucky Derby Daily racing.

True Nicks – A highly specialized operation that has partnered with the Blood Horse LLC and Pedigree Consult LLC. The programs use statistical data to target a variety of information associated with Pedigree History, Breeding Awards, Lifetime Sire Records and Trainer Statistics.

Blood Horse & **Blood Horse Daily** – A wonderful racing magazine published monthly and daily that delivers vital information about horse sales at many different localities. It has timely stories about upcoming and past racing events. Photos of horses, owners, trainers and jockeys are world class. Many up-to-date articles dealing with horse performance in stakes races surely please the reader.

US Racing News and Handicapping Reports – A U.S. Racing Service featuring Thoroughbred, Harness and Greyhound betting content. The service covers over 200 racetracks in the U.S., Europe and Asia. In the U.S., horse betting is available on track and online in various forms. Information includes race analyses, racehorse winners, free handicapping tips and stories on owners, trainers and jockeys.

Paulick Report - This report is an online program featuring a wide variety of information about Bloodlines, Racetrack Industry, Kentucky Derby events, and other great stories about racing and management of thoroughbreds. In addition, the "Ask Ray" allows a special exchange of communication between Ray and fans with questions.

CHAPTER 7

FACTORS AFFECTING WINS

The Kentucky Derby race starts on the First Saturday of May. Up to 14 races may be scheduled for the day. The first race begins at 10:30 a.m. The post time for the Kentucky Derby is usually around 6:30 p.m.

As the horses enter the track from the paddock, the fans begin singing the famous song "**My Old Kentucky Home, Good Night**" written by Stephen C. Foster.[1] Foster composed the song in 1852 and it was published in New York in 1853. The song became the Kentucky State Official Song in 1928. The Louisville Marching Band first played it at the 1921 or the 1930 Kentucky Derby.

These are some of the original lyrics of Stephen C. Foster's famous song.

The sun shines bright in the old Kentucky home.
'Tis summer, the people are gay,
The corn top's ripe and the meadow's in the bloom
While the birds make music all the day.
The young folks roll on the little cabin floor,
All merry, all happy, and bright.
By 'n by hard times comes a-knocking at the door,
Then my old Kentucky home, good night.

Weep no more my lady, oh! weep no more today!
We will sing one song for the old Kentucky home,
For the old Kentucky home far away.

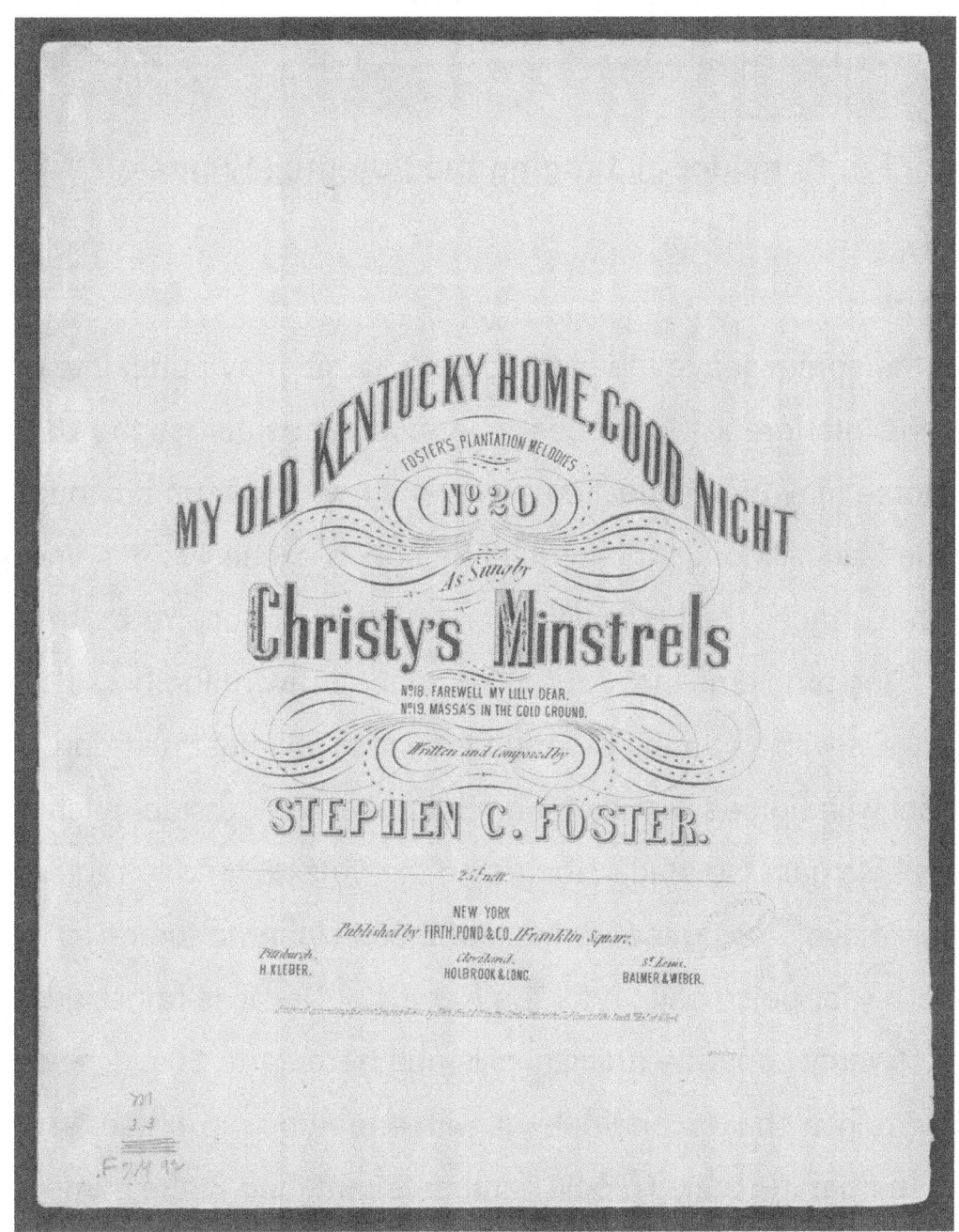

Copy of the Front Cover of the Original Song "My Old Kentucky Home, Good Night" Composed by Stephen Collins Foster in 1852 and Published in 1853. (Library of Congress)

Racing officials plan for a Derby field of 20 horses each year. The largest field has been 23 in 1974 and he smallest field 3 in 1892 and 1905.

Factors to Consider in Judging the Potential Winner.

Post Position

After the horses leave the starting gate, some may bump into one another. If the interference is excessive in most races across the U. S. the offending horse may be disqualified and placed behind from any number of horses in the field. Although the contact has been excessive in some Kentucky Derby races, no disqualifications have ever occurred.

Part of the problems may be related to the draw of the horse's post position. Horses with low numbers near the inner rail must rush forward to avoid contact with horses with high numbers near the outside rail that cross over suddenly to gain the lead. Horses on the outside tend to require more effort earlier to avoid being too far back of those closer to the rail.

The draw for post position for the Kentucky Derby is rather arbitrarily conducted. Twenty separate artificial pills numbered 1 to 20 are placed in a pill bag. The bag is shaken and one pill with one number printed on it is shaken loose from the bag. The pill number is matched to the same number printed on a sheet bearing the name of the horse printed on it. The number on the pill becomes the assigned post position for the horse. The horse's name is matched with the number of the pill drawn. The draw occurs a few days earlier than the race. Trainers and jockeys use this time to arrange for differences in strategy or changes associated with the horse.

Also, the track handicapper uses the assigned starting position to set the odds for each horse.

The horse's starting position in the gate potentially affects the trainer/jockey strategy and race outcome. The starting gate system for the Derby race dates to 1930.[2] Two gates are coupled, the main near the inner rail holds 14 horses and an auxiliary gate near the outer rail holds six more horses. For extra starting space, some trainers and jockeys prefer a post position just outside the main gate. A problem exists if the gates are misaligned at the turn. This difference needs to be corrected.

Racing on the first turn creates problems. Horses racing on the outside are less likely to bump, but may race too far wide instead. Data show turns in the Derby account for approximately 40 percent of the 1 ¼-mile race. Calculations argue that a horse racing outside would need to run farther because of the thickness of the bodies of the horse and jockey. A horse racing further out from the inner rail would race significantly more than a horse near the inner rail. Also, it's quite difficult for a jockey weighing 110 lb. or less to handle a 1,200 lb. horse racing at full gallop.

Over the course of Derby history, the post positions with the greatest number of wins are 9 and 10. Just four have won beyond position 16. Comparison of winners over the past 56 years shows horses with post positions 4 - 7 have won four times and horses 10 -16, six times. None has won from position 3 in 20 years. None has ever won from position 17.

The average field size over the years has been 13.5 horses. Since 2000 it has been 19, with the least at 16. Nine of the 18 winners since 2000 broke from post position 13 or higher. Previous records of 70 races show 10 winners broke from post position 13 or higher.

On May 1, 2018, Newsday.com listed some of the winners based on post position since 1930[3] and Jody Demling, America's Best Racing[4] as:

1 — 8 winners

Ferdinand (1986); Chateaugay (1963); Needles (1956); Hill Gail (1952); Citation (1948); Gallahadion (1940); Lawrin (1938); War Admiral (1937).

2 — 7 winners

Affirmed (1978); Bold Forbes (1976); Cannonade (1974); Dust Commander (1970); Tim Tam (1958); Ponder; (1949) Assault (1946).

3 — 5 winners

Real Quiet (1998); Alysheba (1987); Spectacular Bid (1979); Foolish Pleasure (1975); Shut Out (1942).

4 — 5 winners

Super Saver (2010); Seattle Slew (1977); Decidedly (1962); Pensive (1944); Whirlaway (1941).

5 — 10 winners

Always Dreaming (2017); California Chrome (2014), Funny Cide (2003); War Emblem (2002); Silver Charm (1997); Strike the Gold (1991); Count Fleet (1943); Johnstown (1939); Bold Venture (1936); Twenty Grand (1931).

6 — 2 winners

Sea Hero (1993); Iron Leige (1957)

7 — 7 winners

Justify (2018); Street Sense (2007); Pleasant Colony (1981); Proud Clarion (1967); Northern Dancer (1964); Determine (1954); Gallant Fox (1930).

8 — 8 winners

Mine That Bird (2009); Barbaro (2006); Go for Gin (1994); Unbridled (1990); Majestic Prince (1969); Lucky Debonair (1965); Swaps (1955); Cavalcade (1934).

9 — 4 winners

Riva Ridge (1972); Venetian Way (1960); Tomy Lee (1959); Count Turf (1951).

10 — 9 winners

Giacomo (2005); Lil E. Tee (1992); Sunday Silence (1989); Spend a Buck (1985); Sunny's Halo (1983); Genuine Risk (1980); Secretariat (1973); Dark Star (1953); Omaha (1935).

11 — 2 winners

Winning Colors (1988); Brokers Tip (1933).

12 — 3 winners

Canonero II (1971); Kauai King (1966); Hoop Jr. (1945)

13 — 5 winners

Nyquist (2016); Smarty Jones (2004); Forward Pass (1968); Jet Pilot (1947); Burgoo King (1932).

14 — 2 winners

Carry Back (1961); Middleground (1950).

15 — 3 winners

Fusaichi Pegasus (2000); Grindstone (1996); Swale (1984).

16 — 5 winners

Orb (2013); Animal Kingdom (2011); Monarchos (2001); Charismatic (1999); Thunder Gulch (1995).

17 — 0 winners

18 — 2 winners

American Pharoah (2015); Gato Del Sol (1982).

19 — 1 winner

I'll Have Another (2012).

20 — 1 winner

Big Brown (2008).

These records show no winners from post positions 1 and 2 in the past 32 years and one winner from post position 3 in the past 20 years.

Some consideration needs to be made for horses positioned close to the inner rail and the outer far rail. These horses are poor bets to win.

Fastest Kentucky Derbys and Post Position

There is little chance of a new entrant breaking the current track record for the 1-1/4 - mile Kentucky Derby. Secretariat ran the fastest Kentucky Derby, a record that has stood for 45 years. Monarchos ran the second fastest time and that is 17 years ago. Comparison of winners over the past 56 years shows horses with post positions 4 - 7 won four times and horses 10 -16, six times. No horse has run faster from the 1 or 2 positions in 32 years.

Here are the fastest Kentucky Derbies and post positions since 1962.[5,6] The horses raced over a track labeled fast.

1973 – Secretariat – 1:59.40; #10

2001 – Monarchos – 1:59.97; #16

1964 - Northern Dancer – 2:00.00; #7

1985 – Spend A Buck – 2:00.10; #10

1962 – Decidedly – 2:00.40; #4

1967 – Proud Clarion – 2:00.60; #7

1998 – Grindstone – 2:01.06; #15

2000 – Fusaichi Pegasus – 2:01.12 #15

2003 – Funny Cide – 2:01.19 #5

1995 – Thunder Gulch – 2:01.20 #16

Favorite at Post time

The track handicapper, certain racing analysts and the general public have been pretty good at selecting recent winners. Six winners have been favorites for the past six years: Justify (2018); Always Dreaming (2017); Nyquist (2016); American Pharoah (2015); California Chrome (2014); and Orb (2013).

State and Stakes Race For Previous Victories 2000-2018

Most races held within a month or so prior to the Kentucky Derby usually result in the most successful racing performance of the horse in the Kentucky Derby. The reasons for this outcome are primarily associated with fitness of the horse. Most of the grand performers have been raced into condition that allows for the best outcome. The following races held nearest the post-time start include the Florida Derby, Santa Anita Derby, Wood Memorial, Blue Grass Stakes and Arkansas Derby.

Florida tops other states with horses holding the most recent victories. Thirteen of the recent wins have occurred in states other than Kentucky, the key playground of thoroughbred racing. The records show:

Florida – 6 - Florida Derby

2017 - Always Dreaming

2016 - Nyquist

2013 - Orb

2008 - Big Brown

2006 - Barbaro

2001 - Monarchos

California – 4 - Santa Anita Derby

2018 - Justify

2014 - California Chrome

2012 - I'll Have Another

2005 - Giacomo – Finished fourth

Arkansas – 3 - Arkansas Derby

2015 - American Pharaoh

2010 - Super Saver

2004 - Smarty Jones

Kentucky – 2 - Blue Grass & Spiral Stakes

2011 – Animal Kingdom – Spiral

2007 – Street Sense – Blue Grass – Finished second

New York – 2 - Wood Memorial

2000 – Fusaichi Pegasus

2003 – Funny Cide – Finished second

Illinois – 1 - Illinois Derby

2002 - War Emblem

New Mexico – 1 - Sunland Derby

2009 – Mine That Bird

Condition of Track Surface

Another factor to consider is the condition of the track. Does it make a difference if the track is dry, sloppy or muddy? Are some horses more likely to perform better on one type of track condition than another?

Whenever a horse has made his most recent start on a muddy track, handicappers have to judge whether his performance was a true gauge of his ability or whether it was significantly affected by the racing surface. This is an issue of special relevance in the 138th Preakness, because many of the entrants raced over a sloppy track in the Kentucky Derby, with three of them losing by 20 lengths or more. Can these horses be expected to run much better on a fast track at the Pimlico Race Course?

After 1945, the Kentucky Derby has been run 11 times on a track officially labeled **sloppy, muddy or slow.** The winning horses are: Justify (2018 - 2:04.20); Orb (2013 - 2:02.89); Super Saver (2010 - 2:04.45);Mine That Bird (2009 - 2:02.66); Smarty Jones (2004 - 2:04.06; Go for Gin (1994 - 2:03 2/5); Sunday Silence (1989 - 2:05); Tim Tam(1958 - 2:05); Citation (1948 - 2:05 2/5); Jet Pilot (1947 - 2:06-4/5) and Assault (1946 - 2;06 4/5). Comparison of times shows that Mine That Bird ran the fastest time. All horses raced over 2:02.

In five of those years, the winner of the Derby went on to capture the Preakness.[7] In two of the other years, the Preakness was won by a horse who didn't start in the Derby. The Derby losers who triumphed at Pimlico were: Lookin at Lucky, 6th in the 2010 Derby; Tabasco Cat, 6th in the 1994 Derby; and Faultless, 3rd in the 1947 Derby.

Lookin at Lucky had a difficult trip from post position one so the sloppy track can't account for the poor performance. Faultless raced well in the mud and lost the Derby in a close photo finish. Beaten by 9 1/2 lengths, Tabasco Cat lost the Derby and ran with the slower horses. Still, he performed poorly in the mud with this group.

An article published in the 2013 The Washington Post showed that the horses tend to race slower on an off track than on a fast track.[5] The results (below) show winners of the Kentucky Derby that raced on and off track went on to win the Preakness Stakes two weeks later.

YEAR	DERBY WIN	PREAKNESS WIN (DERBY FINISH)
2018	Justify	Justify
2010	Super Saver	Lookin at Lucky (6th)
2009	Mine That Bird	Rachel Alexandra (DNS)
2004	Smarty Jones	Smarty Jones
1994	Go for Gin	Tabasco Cat (6th)
1989	Sunday Silence	Sunday Silence
1958	Tim Tam	Tim Tam
1948	Citation	Citation
1947	Jet Pilot	Faultless (3rd)
1946	Assault	Assault

During the first 75 years (1883-1958), 22 (29.3 %) have been listed as offtrack conditions. In the past 29 years (199-2018), seven (24.1%) have been considered off tracks, sloppy-2018 (Justify), 2013 (Orb), 2010 (Super

Saver), 2009 (Mine That Bird), 2004 (Smarty Jones), 1994 (Go for Gin) and muddy-1989 (Sunday Silence).

Considering the Derby winners and the performances of Preakness winner's two weeks later shows that the wet track in Kentucky has little to do with the finishing outcome in the Preakness.

Racing as Two-Year Olds

Just two horses have won the Kentucky Derby without having raced as a two-year old. Apollo won in 1882 when the Derby was contested at 1—1/2 miles. Jenna West, Sports Illustrated, 2018 reported that Justify broke the "Apollo Curse" after 126 years winning at 1-1/4 miles in 2018.[8]

Horses Bred/Foaled Outside the U.S.

Omar Khayam won the Kentucky Derby in 1917. Foaled in England, he won by two lengths over Ticket in a time of 2:04.35. Two horses bred in Canada have won, namely Northern Dancer and Sunny's Halo. Northern Dancer's dam, Natalma, was bred to Nearactic at Oshawa, Canada. In 1964, Northern Dancer beat Hill Rise in a time of 2:00 flat. Bred and foaled in Canada, 1983 winner Sunny's Halo won the 1983 Kentucky Derby winning over Desert Wine in a time of 2:02.1/5. British bred Tomy Lee beat Sword Dancer by a nose in 1959 in a time of 2:02.20.

Workouts

Proper, regular exercise is vital to success of the racing horse. The problem is just how often, far and hard should the workout be conducted.

Generally speaking, a horse is considered reasonably fit if it races at least once a month. The trainer may try to sharpen its performance by adding a workout in between. This style of management has become common among horses of stakes caliber.

Review of the 20 horses entered in the 2018 Kentucky Derby showed no horse had a timed workout within a week before the Derby. Two weeks prior to the Derby, 15 had worked twice with an interval of 6-8 days in between. Three had raced within 21 days preceding Derby race week.

Once lightly raced horses become familiar with surroundings of the track, trainers work them every two weeks or so depending on track conditions. Trainers presume that a workout time prior to a race gives some idea of the expected performance in the coming race. Whether this is useful is questionable for a horse racing the 1-1/4 -mile Derby. Most of the 2018 Derby entrants worked either four or five furlongs (1/2 or 5/8 mile) two weeks before the Derby. Six horses worked much faster than other horses that worked on the same day. For example, Promises Fulfilled ran 4th fastest out of a total of 55; Flameaway 2/55; Enticed 2/7; Instilled Regard 3/62; Magnum Moon 4/75; and Vino Rossi 1/75. These horses performed so poorly in the Derby that these intensive workouts must not have helped them run faster. In comparison, two of the top three finishers did not have a fast workout. The second placed finisher Good Magic ran 8/55 breezing; third place finisher Audible 39/75 breezing. and Justify, the winner, had worked a speedy 7 furlongs in 1:25 handily. These differences suggest that competitiveness in a race previous to the Derby might be more beneficial than speed training.

Track Confirmation

Kentucky Derby starters race over the dirt track at Churchill Downs. They start at the head of the stretch near the ¼ marker and race pass the finish line in front of the grandstand. They circle the Clubhouse turn and then race along the backside. Near the ½ mile marker, they start to accelerate to gain position. As they enter the stretch, they drive toward the finish line.

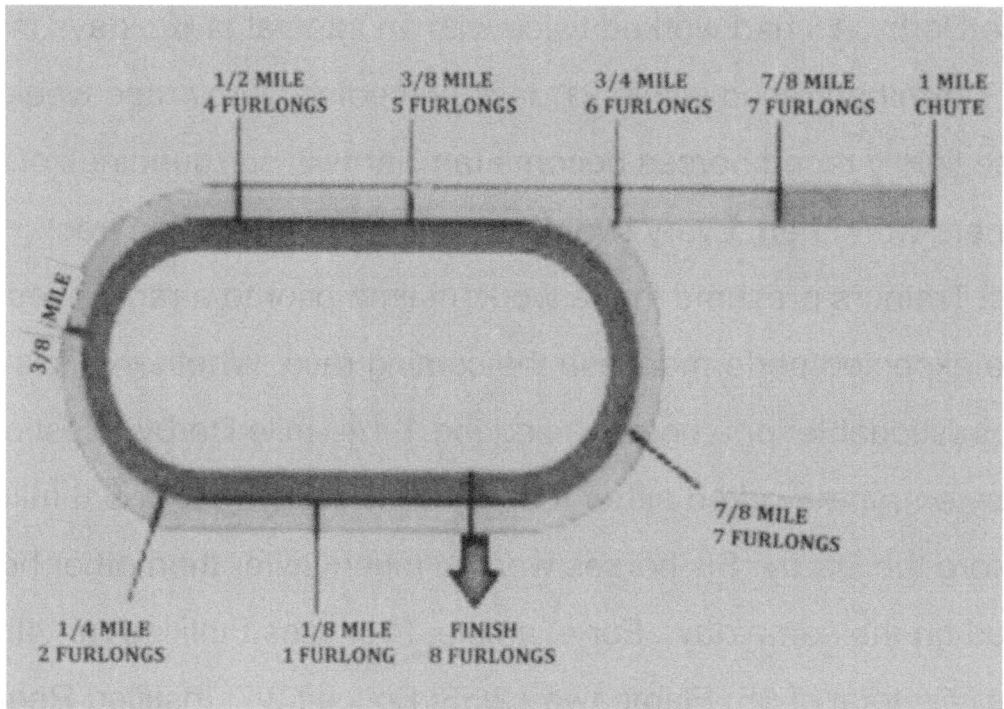

Churchill Downs – 1 Mile Track Shown with Furlong Markers - Derby Starting Gate is Located at the 1/4 Mile Marker at Head of Stretch, Horses Race Around the Clubhouse Turn and Then Race Past the 1/4 Marker Again on the Way to the Finish Line.

Lasix or Not

At most tracks across the country nearly all horses race on Lasix. This medication is given because the horses tend to undergo excessive lung bleeding caused by heavy breathing during racing.

When horses are given Lasix, race performance has been shown to improve, but it does not always control bleeding.[9] Because horses urinate more frequently when given Lasix, current regulations require that it not be administered on race day.

Gender of Horse

Three-year old males having testicles are termed colts. Three-year-old males without testicles are termed geldings. If the testicles fail to descend, they are called ridglings. Three-year old females are called fillies.

The records show most of the winning horses are colts. Nine winning geldings include: Mine that Bird (2009); Funny Cide (2003); Clyde Van Dusen (1929); Paul Jones (1920); Exterminator (1918); Old Rosebud (1914); Macbeth II (1888); Apollo (1882); and Vagrant (1876).

Thirty-nine fillies have started in the Kentucky Derby and three have won. These are: Winning Colors (1988); Genuine Risk (1980) and Regret (1915).

Jody Demling, Louisville Courier Journal, May 5, 2018 covered the outcome of the 2008 Kentucky Derby.[10] She described the incident that Eight Belles finished second and had broken down. The filly had to be humanely euthanized on the track after the finish. She had broken both cannon and sesamoid bones in the lower front legs. No treatment was attempted because the injuries were too severe.

CHAPTER 8

FAMOUS OWNERS

It is doubtful that any person or group racing under the same name will surpass the record of eight times that Calumet Farm has won the Kentucky Derby. The next closest is E. R. Bradley who is deceased. Belair Stud Farm has closed. Probably the remainder will never race enough to catch up. Thus, any future change might come from a winning owner of the past 20 years.

According to Horse Racing Nation,[1] some names include:

Calumet Farm – 8 (Forward Pass 1968); (Tim Tam 1958); (Iron Liege 1957); (Hill Gail 1952); (Ponder 1949); (Citation 1948); (Pensive 1944); Whirlaway 1941). [2,3]

Colonel Edward R. Bradley – 4 (Brokers Tip 1933); (Burgoo King 1932); (Bubbling Over 1926); (Behave Yourself 1921).[4,5]

Belair Stud – 3 (Johnstown 1939); (Omaha 1935); (Gallant Fox 1930).[6,7]

Bashford Manor Stable – 2 (Sir Huon 1906); (Azra 1892).[8]

Harry Payne Whitney – 2 (Whiskery 1927); (Regret 1915).[9,10]

John & Fannie Hertz - 2 (Count Fleet 1943); (Reigh Count 1928).[11,12]

Greentree Stable – 2 (Shut Out 1942); (Twenty Grand 1931).[13,14]

King Ranch – 2 (Middleground 1950); (Assault 1946).[15,16]

Darby Dan Farm – 2 (Proud Clarion 1967); (Chateaugay 1963).[17,18]

Meadow Stable – 2 (Secretariat 1973); (Riva Ridge 1972).[19,20]

Bob & Beverly Lewis – 2 (Charismatic 1999); (Silver Charm 1997)[21,22]

J. Paul Reddam - 2 (Nyquist 2016); (I'll Have Another 2012)[23,24]

Calumet Farm (8): It's highly unlikely that any other owner (s) will ever become as successful in winning the Kentucky Derby as Calumet Farm. The famous tract of land borders the Versailles Road near Lexington, Kentucky. And most winners have been bred there. A strange outcome came with the victory in the 1968 Derby. Forward Pass, one of the eight bred at the farm received it through a disqualification. Dancer's Image, bred elsewhere, crossed the finish line first, but was disqualified for having received an injection of unlawful medication termed phenylbutazone (Bute) in his system. Calumet bred 1991 Derby winner, Strike the Gold, but did not own him when he raced.

The farm of 767 acres has had several owners over the years. But all Kentucky Derby winners belonged to members of the William Wright family. William Wright, founder of Calumet Baking Powder, acquired the property in 1924 and started a Standard Bred breeding operation. He died in 1932 and his son, Warren Wright and his wife, Lucille operated the farm for breeding and racing thoroughbreds. After Warren's death, Lucille got control of the farm in 1950 and married Gene Markey in 1952. She died in 1982 and operation of the farm went to the husband of Wright's eldest child. In 1992, businessman Henryk de Kwiatkowski bought the farm. He died in 2003 leaving the farm under control of family members. The Calumet Investment Group bought the property and has leased it to Brad Kelly, the fourth largest U. S. landowner. Kelly races/breeds thoroughbreds using the name of Calumet Farm

Colonel Edward R. Bradley (4): Bradley, born in Pennsylvania, spent much time gambling and racing horses. After moving to Texas, he became a bookmaker operating in Memphis, St Louis and Hot Springs. He moved to Chicago and bought a hotel, then moved to Palm Beach and opened a casino, the Palmetto Club. He bought the Fair Grounds Race Course in New Orleans after earning money from an investment in the Hialeah Race Course, Miami. He bought a thoroughbred in 1898 and then acquired the Ash Grove Stock Farm near Lexington, Kentucky. In 1906, he changed the name to Idle Hour Farm and began racing and breeding thoroughbreds. He named his thoroughbreds starting with "B" letters. Among his Stakes winners, four won the Kentucky Derby, three the Preakness Stakes, and two, the Belmont Stakes.

An established philanthropist, he donated funds to orphans, hospitals and the city of Palm Beach. In 2000, the Florida Department of State named him "One of the Great Floridians."

Belair Stud (3): Belair Stud Farm, Bowie, Maryland, had some great horses in the 1930's-50's. James T. Woodward developed the farm in 1907 and operated a breeding-racing stable that lasted until 1957. Belair Mansion and a two-acre plat northeast remains as part of the stable grounds.

The Belair Mansion Museum is operated by the City of Bowie and has been recognized by the National Register of Historic Places. Triple Crown Winners Gallant Fox and Omaha remain as the only father-son combination in Triple Crown history. Nashua, second to Swaps in the 1955 Kentucky Derby, became the "Horse of the Year" after defeating Swaps in a match race at Washington Park in 1955. He won the Preakness and Belmont Stakes in 1955. Sold to the owners of Spendthrift Farm, Lexington, Kentucky he stood stud duty at the farm and died at age 30.

Bashford Manor Stud (2): Bashford Manor Farm, located on Bardstown Road, West Buechel, Kentucky started as a tract of 1,000 acres. George Wilder developed the farm and had a house (Bashford Manor Estate) built on it in 1871-1872. In 1882, George James Long purchased the property and organized a breeding/racing stable. He became the Master of Bashford Manor Stud Farm. Under the name of Bashford Manor, he raced four horses in the Derby 1891-1894. His Azra won in 1892. Between 1895-1908, he raced six other horses under the name of George J. Long. His Sir Huon won in 1906. He bred 1899 Derby winner Manuel, but did not own him. On September 23, 1918, the Thoroughbred Record reported that George J. Long had survived a stroke. In 1951, the Buechel's Women's Club bought the home, but never restored it. The Louisville Trust Bank assumed control of it and built a branch office on the corner of the property. In 1973, the bank sold the building to George J. Long's two grandsons. They had the house demolished in 1973. The current residential neighborhood has a shopping mall.

Harry Payne Whitney - 2: Harry Payne Whitney entered 20 horses in the Kentucky Derby beginning in 1915 through 1927. He won with Regret in 1915, the first filly to do so. Named "Horse of the Year," she held the filly record until 1980 when Genuine Risk became the second filly to win. In 1927, Whitney's Whiskery pulled the trick. His 3-year old colt Upset, finished second in the 1920 Derby. He became the only horse to defeat the great Man O' War, but not in the Derby. His colt, Prudery, finished third in 1921 Derby.

Whitney inherited his love for thoroughbred racing from his wealthy father William C. Whitney, Secretary of the Navy. He bred 191 stakes winners from 1905 through 1930. Recognized as a prominent New York polo player, he married the famous New York sculptor Gertrude Vanderbilt in 1896. She belonged to the wealthy Vanderbilt family. Their son, Cornelius Vanderbilt Whitney owner of the C.V. Whitney Farm, Lexington, Kentucky won many top races and bred at least 175 stakes winners.

John D and Fannie Hertz (2): Francis "Fannie" Kerner Hertz bought Reigh Count as a 2-year old. Foaled at New Market, Virginia, he won the Kentucky Derby and became "Horse of the Year" in 1928. John Daniel Hertz.Sr. born in Slovakia moved to Chicago at age 5 years. He married Fannie in 1903 and began selling automobiles for a friend. Hertz started the

Yellow Cab Company and Checker Cab Company in Chicago. Later, he bought a rental car company, calling it Hertz Drive-Ur-Self Corporation.

Hertz and Fannie bought Stoner Creek Stud Farm at Paris, Kentucky in the 1930's. Reigh Count's son Count Fleet, foaled at Stoner Creek Stud Farm in 1940, won the Triple Crown in 1943.

Count Turf, by Count Fleet a son of Reigh Count, won the 1951 Kentucky Derby. Bred by Dr. & Mrs. Frank P. Miller and raised at Runnymeade Farm, Paris, Kentucky, Jack Amiel a New York restauranteur bought him at a yearling auction.

Greentree Stable (2): William Payne Whitney and wife Helen Julia Hay Whitney had a strong interest in breeding and racing horses. Payne started racing steeplechase horses in 1911 by winning the Greentree Cup at Great Neck, New York. The couple organized the Greentree Stable at Red Bank, New Jersey in 1914. They owned horse farms at Saratoga, New York and Aiken, South Carolina and developed a thoroughbred nursery in Lexington, Kentucky in 1925.

Under the title of Greentree Farm, Payne entered 14 horses in the Kentucky Derby. He entered a colt named Letterman in his first in 1922. In 1923, the couple raced Rialto and Cherry Pie against brother Harry's Enchantment and Picketer. After William Payne died in 1927, Helen and her family members ran the racing operations. Two winners, Twenty Grand in 1931 and Shut Out in 1942, formed part of the group that won seven Triple Crown races, including the Kentucky Derby.

John Hay Whitney, son of the couple, owned Mare's Nest Farm and inherited Greentree Farm in 1944. A section of the Lexington nursery sold to Gainesway Farm.

King Ranch (2): King Ranch occupies 825,000 acres between Corpus Christi and Brownsville near Kingsville, Texas. Owner Robert Kleberg acquired the southern part of Idle Hour Stock Farm, Old Frankfort Pike, at Lexington, Kentucky following the death of owner Colonel E. R. Bradley in 1945. The property became King Ranch's Kentucky Division of Thoroughbred racing. It sold in the 1980's.

Kleberg bought 1936 Kentucky Derby and Preakness winner Bold Venture in 1939 from Martin Swartz at Saratoga Springs, New York. Foaled at the Texas ranch, Assault, son of Bold Venture won the Kentucky Derby and Belmont Stakes in 1946. Middleground, another son of Bold Venture, won the Kentucky Derby and the Belmont Stakes in 1950.

Darby Dan Farm (2): John W. Galbreath, born Derby, Ohio, formed a successful thoroughbred operation in Darby Dan Farm, Galloway, Ohio, 1935. In 1949, he bought 650 acres of the former Idle Hour Stud Farm, Old Frankford Pike, Lexington, Kentucky. An imaginative selector of fine thoroughbreds, he imported the undefeated racer, Ribot from Europe. Over the years he bred Graustark by Robot, arranged for breeding of Swaps and lease of an imported sire, Sea-Bird. Some of his famous racers included His Majesty, Little Current "Three-year-Old of the Year" and Sword Dancer racing's "Horse of Year." His Roberto won the English Derby in 1972. He received the Eclipse Award for Breeders in 1972. Chateaugay (1963) and Proud Clarion (1967) won the Kentucky Derby in two of the fastest times, 2:01.4/5 and 2:00.1/5.

Meadow Stable (2): Christopher T. Chenery, a native Virginian, spent part of his life as an engineer in New Rochelle, New York. He and daughter, Penny born at New Rochelle, raised and trained famous thoroughbreds at The Meadow, Doswell, Virginia. Christopher acquired the farm from an ancestor Charles Dabney Morris.

The Chenery family kept at least 15 well-bred mares on the farm during the 1950s-1960's. They raced four horses in the Kentucky Derby, including Hill Prince, 2nd in 1950; First Landing 3rd in 1959; Riva Ridge 1st in 1972 and Secretariat 1st in 1973. Riva Ridge coasted to victory in 2:01.4/5 and Secretariat set the existing track record of 1:59.2/5.

Bob and Beverly Lewis (2): The couple began thoroughbred racing in 1990 and continued for 10 years. Their horses won 50 stakes races. Bob, born in Minneapolis, grew up in Glendale, California. He married Beverly who was attending the University of Oregon. While working in California brewery, he later became one of the leading distributors for Anheuser-Busch in the U. S. In 1990, the couple bought Timber Country that finished third in the Kentucky Derby. They won the Kentucky Derby and Preakness with Silver Charm and Preakness (1997) and Charismatic (1999). Silver Charm beat Captain Bodgit by a head in the Derby and became Champion "Three-Year Colt of 1997." Commendable won the 1990 Belmont Stakes. They owned and raced Champion "Three-Year-Old Filly", Serena's Song.

J. Paul Reddam – Born in Windsor, Canada, Reddam moved to California and obtained a Ph.D. from the University of Southern California. He became a businessman and University Professor in Los Angeles. He founded Ditech, a mortgage lending company, and sold it to General Motors. He currently owns CashCall, Inc., a lending company.

He developed an interest in harness racing while living in Canada. He owned a Standardbred business in Windsor and also in Cal Expo,

Sacramento, California.

In 1988, he entered thoroughbred racing and won the 2014 Kentucky Derby with I'll Have Another that broke from the 19th post position. His thoroughbred, Nyquist won the 2016 Kentucky Derby. Doug O'Neill manages the training of the 40 horses in the J. Paul Reddam Racing Stable, L.L.C.

CHAPTER 9

LEADING TRAINERS

It takes considerable experience and good luck just to get the opportunity to train a horse with appropriate credentials to enter the Kentucky Derby. To win is an amazing, thrilling and fantastic experience. A few living trainers have conditioned more than one winner. Some others have passed away and some others who remain have retired.

Trainers With Two Or More Wins

Ben Jones - 6 (Hill Gail 1952); Ponder (1949); Citation (1948); Pensive (1944); Whirlaway (1941) and Lawrin (1938) from 1909 -1953. He trained five of the six while working at Calumet Farm. Ben became semi-retired after 1946 and gets credit for the last three winners. H. A."Jimmy" Jones, son, did most of the training after that. He won with Tim Tam in 1958 and Iron Liege in 1957.[1,2] **Deceased**

Bob Baffert – 5 (Justify 2018); (American Pharoah 2015); (War Emblem 2002); (Real Quiet 1998); (Silver Charm 1997). He has entered 28 starters and some have finishes second or third. He has trained winners of 16 Triple Crown races, including 11 champions to win a total of 15 Eclipse Awards. Five of his Kentucky Derby winners won the Preakness. Justify and American Pharoah won the Triple Crown. Baffert is also a member of the Horse Racing Hall of Fame.[3,4] **Active**

D. Wayne Lukas – 4 (Charismatic 1999); Grindstone 1996); (Thunder Gulch 1995); (Winning Colors 1988). He has entered 48 horses to run in the Derby. He began training in 1974 and has trained the most champions in racing history. His horses dominated racing in the 1980's and 90's. His legacy lives through other successful trainers namely Todd Pletcher, Kieran McLaughlin, and Dallas Stewart. Lukas is a member of the Horse Racing Hall of Fame.[5,6] **Active**

Herbert J. Thompson – 4 (Brokers Tip 1933); (Burgoo King 1932); Bubbling Over 1926) (Behave Yourself 1921). Thompson, a Michigan native, he trained thoroughbreds in the West Coast for E. J. Baldwin. He moved to Kentucky and trained under Colonel E. R. Bradley in Lexington, His four Derby winners remained with Bradley's stable. He won his first Derby at 40 years and the last at 52 years. He had the first and second place finishers twice. Probably his most famous Derby winner was Broker's Tip who beat Head Play in the infamous "Fighting Finish" Derby of 1933.[7] **Deceased**

James E "Sunny James" Fitzsimmons – 3 (Johnstown 1939); (Omaha 1935); (Gallant Fox 1930). He started 11 horses in the Derby and won 2,275 races in his career. His two Derby winners came during the time he trained for William Woodward's Belair Stable. He trained for the Phipps Wheatley Stable until the end of his career. Nashua lost the Derby to Swaps in 1955, but became Horse of the Year. He also trained Bold Ruler, sire of the great Secretariat. He won the Leading Trainer Award in Earnings five times.[8] **Deceased**

Max Hirsch – 3 (Middleground 1950); (Assault 1946); (Bold Venture 1936). Known as the famous trainer at King Ranch his career lasted 70 years. He trained Sarazen Horse of the Year in 1924-25, and became the trainer for King Ranch in the 1930's until his death in 1969. Unfortunately, Assault, his Triple Crown winner of 1946, proved infertile.[9] **Deceased**

Nick Zito - 2 (Go for Gin 1994); (Strike the Gold 1991); one second (Ice Box 2010). Zito began training in 1971 and has had 21 Derby starters through 2018. He has also won 1 Preakness and 2 Belmont Stakes, giving him 5 wins, 8 seconds, and 7 thirds from his 61 Triple Crown starters. The two Belmont victories are interesting. His Birdstone defeated Derby-Preakness winner Smarty Jones in 2004, and Da' Tara defeated Derby-Preakness winner Big Brown in 2008. He was inducted into the National Horse Racing Hall of Fame in 2005.[10,11] **Active**

Douglas F. O'Neill – 2 (Nyquist 2016); (I'll Have Another 2012). O'Neill, a Michigan native, got his trainers license in 1989. Since then, he has become an outstanding trainer in the 2000's. He entered two other horses in the Kentucky Derby initially in 2007.[12,13] **Active**

Todd Pletcher- 2- (Always Dreaming 2017); (Super Saver 2010); 3rd (Revolutionary 2013). Born in Texas, he got his trainers license in 1995. He had worked as a groom with D. Wayne Lukas since 1989 and helped in the training of Derby winner Thunder Gulch. He trained numerous other Derby horses in 2015 and 2014. Pletcher has been named Eclipse Award Outstanding Trainer of the year seven times.[14] **Active**

Hall of Fame Trainers – 2 Wins; Retired or Deceased.

Charles Whittingham – (Sunday Silence 1989); (Ferdinand 1986). [15] **Deceased**

Woodford "Woody" Chefs Stephens – (Swale 1984); (Cannonade 1974). [16, 17] **Deceased**

LeRoy Jolley- (Genuine Risk 1980); (Foolish Pleasure 1975). [18,19] **Deceased**

Lazaro Barrera – (Affirmed 1978); (Bold Forbes 1976).[20] **Deceased**

Lucien Laurin – (Secretariat 1973); (Riva Ridge 1972).[21,22] **Deceased**

Henry Forest – (Forward Pass 1968); (Kauai King 1966).[23,24] **Deceased**

Horatio Luro – (Northern Dancer 1964); (Decidedly 1962. [25,] **Deceased**

H.A "Jimmy" Jones – (Tim Tam 1958); (Iron Liege 1957).[26,27] **Deceased**

Carl Nafzger – (Street Sense 2007); (Unbridled 1990).[28,29] **Retired**

Other Prominent Trainers With Derby Experience.

Claude McGaughey III - 1 (Orb 2013) A native of Lexington, Kentucky, he won with Orb in 2013. A full - time trainer since 1979, he began training for the Ogden Phipps Stable and has won over 240 graded stakes races. He received the Eclipse Award as Outstanding Trainer in 1988 and the National Horse Racing Hall of Fame in 2004.[30,31] **Active**

H. Graham Motion 1 - (Animal Kingdom 2011) An Englishman, he received his license in 1993 after training under dynamic trainers Johnathan Shepard from 1985 and Bernie Bond 1991. He raced 4th (Went the Way Well) and 15th (Adriano) in the 2012 Derby. His horses have made 12,881 starts with 2,351 wins.[32,33] **Active**

Dale Romans - Born in Louisville, received his license in 1987 and began full time training around 1996. Two of his horses finished 3rd in the Kentucky Derby (Dullahan 2012) and (Paddy O'Prado 2010) and 16th (Free Drop Billy 2018). He received the Eclipse Award 2012 as Outstanding Trainer and is the all-time leadings winning trainer at Churchill Downs with 703 wins and 42 Stakes wins. He has started 12,874 horses with 1,997 wins.[34,35] **Active**

Stephen Asmussen A South Dakota native, his horse (Gun Runner 2016) finished 3rd (Looking at Lee 2015) and (Nehru 2011) both finished 2nd in the Kentucky Derby. He has received the Eclipse Award in 2008 and 2009 and the National Horse Racing Hall of Fame Award. Licensed in 1987. He has been the all-time leading U. S. trainer nine times.[36] **Active**

Chad C. Brown - Licensed in New York in 2007, he has 1 second (Good Magic 2012); 5th (Practical Joke 2017) and 11th (My Man Sam 2016) in the Kentucky Derby. Recipient of the Eclipse Award in 2016, he trained under the famous trainers Claude McGaughey III and Robert Frankel.[37] **Active**

J. Larry Jones - A Hopkinsville, Kentucky native, he received his license in 1982. His (Eight Belles 2009) and (Hard Spun 2007) both finished second in the Kentucky Derby. He had two other entrants in 2009. He has trained horses making 5,659 starts with 1,122 wins.[38] **Active.**

Kenneth McPeek - Born in Arkansas and reared in Lexington, Kentucky, he received his license in 1985. His Derby contact relates to 3rd placed finisher Curlin in the 2007 Derby. Overall, Curlin has earned the most money of any race horse at $10,501,800 million. McPeek has 1,480 wins overall.[39,40] **Active**

Ian Wilkes - From Australia, now lives in Louisville. He trained under important Derby winning trainer Carl Nafzger. He served as regular training rider of 1990 Derby winner Unbridled. He was key associate with Nafzger during the training and racing of Street Sense winner of the 2007 Derby. As of December 2018, his earnings are $35 million with 640 total wins.[41,42] **Active**

Mark E. Casse From Indiana, he has trained successfully primarily in Canada. He received a Kentucky license in 1979 and had the following horses finish in the Derby: 13th (Flameaway 2018); 4th (Classic Empire 2017); 5th (Danzig Moon 2015); and 10th (Seaside Retreat 2003).[43,44] **Active**

William I. Mott - Born in South Dakota, he received his license in 1978 and is the second leading winning trainer at Churchill Downs and productive record holder in New York. He ranks second all-time overall to Dale Romans in having at least 272 winners at Churchill Downs racing with one-third the starters as Romans. In spite of this success, he has started few Derby horses, namely 7th (Hofburg 2018); 5th (Hold Me Back 2009); 13th (Court Vision 2008) and 14th (Z Humor 2008). He has won nine racing titles at Saratoga and 10 racing titles at Belmont Park and received the Eclipse Award as leading U. S. trainer in 1995, 1996 and 2011. In 1998, he

was honored by the National Racing Hall of Fame in Saratoga Springs.[45,46]
Active

Michael J. Maker - Son of a Michigan trainer, he set up a public stable in 1991. He trained under outstanding trainer D. Wayne Lukas until 2003 when he opened his own stable. He ran his first Derby long-shot starter 8th (Stately Victor 2003). In 2014, he ran finishers 11th (General a Rod); 16th ((Harry's Holiday) and 19th (Vicar's in Trouble). Unfortunately, his last two starters drew horrible post positions 2 and 1. His other six starters have finished out of the top three positions. An accomplished trainer he has received six Churchill Downs training awards and became the Champion Trainer during the fall meet in 2016.[47,48] **Active**

Brad H. Cox - Born near Churchill Downs, he received his license in 2005. He trained under prominent trainer Dallas Stewart who is a successful protege of D. Wayne Lukas. He has not entered Derby horses, but trains Monomoy Girl that won the 2018 Kentucky Oaks, the day before the Derby. He has lifetime earnings over $41 million dollars.[49,50] **Active**

Top Trainers Listed by Blood Horse, Through 2018.[51]

Name	Starts	WPS	Win %	WPS %
Chad Brown	839	224-176-113	27	61
Steven Asmussen	1,905	401-344-284	21	54
Todd Pletcher	975	215-154-135	22	52
Bob Baffert	348	113 – 53 - 41	32	59
Brad Cox	921	243-152-117	26	56
Mark Casse	1,249	221-181-172	18	46
Michael Maker	1,167	191-163-151	16	43
John Sadler	415	59 - 64 - 63	14	45
Karl Bromberg	1,837	509-329-254	28	59
Peter Miller	584	133-103 - 80	23	54
William Mott	546	79 - 67- 81	14	42
Jason Servis	441	143 – 75 - 69	32	65

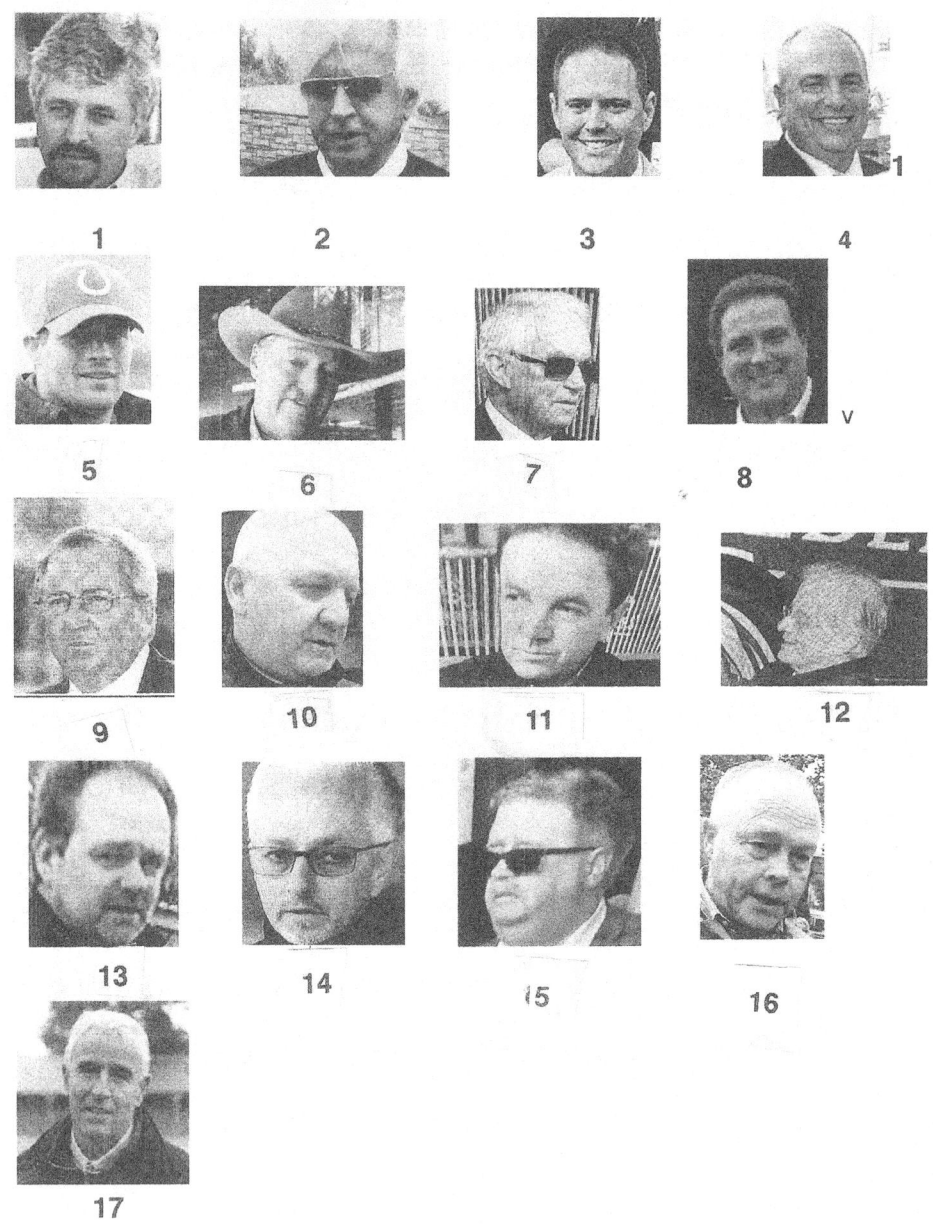

1.Steven Asmussen. 2. Bob Baffert. 3. Chad C. Brown. 4. Mark E. Casse. 5. Brad Cox. 6. J. Larry Jones. 7. D. Wayne Lukas. 8. Michael J. Maker. 9. Claude McGaughey III. 10. Kenneth McPeek. 11. H. Graham Motion. 12. William I. Mott. 13. Douglas F. O'Neill. 14. Todd Pletcher. 15. Dale Romans. 16. Ian Wilkes 17. Nick Zito

CHAPTER 10

WINNING AND OTHER TALENTED JOCKEYS

Jockeys vary in riding style and the years of riding depends much on skill and luck. Some have natural skills and are fortunate to remain healthy. A few attain the highest level of riding and are recognized for their mastery in winning important races such as the Kentucky Derby. Some have won this special event more than once.

George Edward "Eddie" Arcaro – 5 (Hill Gail 1952); (Citation 1948); (Hoop Jr. 1945); (Whirlaway 1941); (Lawrin 1948) in 21 starts. Called "Banana Nose" and "The Master" he is considered one of the all-time greatest jockeys. Elected to the Hall of Fame in 1958, he retired at 46 years with 4,779 wins. He died in Miami, Florida.[1,2] **Deceased**

William John "Bill" HardtackJr. – 5 (Majestic Prince 1969); (Northern Dancer 1964); (Decidedly 1962); Venetian Way 1960); (Iron Leige 1957) for 12 rides in the Kentucky Derby. The Pennsylvania native rode from 1953 at age 21 years. He quit riding in 1974, the last part of the career in Hong Kong. Elected to the Hall of Fame, this marvelous finisher had 4,272 wins. He died in Texas in 2007.[3,4] **Deceased**

William Lee "Bill" Shoemaker – 4 (Ferdinand 1986); (Lucky Debonair 1965); (Tomy Lee 1959); (Swaps 1955) for 26 races from 1952-1988. He lost control of Gallant Man in the 1957 Derby when he stood up before the finish line and Bill Hardtack on Iron Liege passed him. He became the oldest jockey to win the Derby when he rode Ferdinand to win in 1986. Born in Texas, he rode for the fist time at age 18 years and had 8,833 wins during his career. He retired in 1990, became a trainer and died at 72 years in California.[5,6] **Deceased**

Isaac Burns Murphy – 3 - Murphy won with (Kingman 1891); (Riley 1890); and (Buchanan 1884) in 11 Kentucky Derby mounts. He finished second once and third twice. He began riding at age 16 years and won 628 of 1,412 races in a career that ended at his death in 1896. Another report of his record states he won 530 races on 1,538 mounts. An African American, he won the Kentucky Derby, Kentucky Oaks and the Clark Handicap in the same year 1884, the only jockey ever to do so. Elected to the National Thoroughbred Racing Hall of Fame, he was called the "Colored Archer", a name he acquired from comparison to an English rider named Archer.[7,8] **Deceased**

Earl Harold Sande - 3 – A former bronco buster, Sande won aboard (Gallant Fox 1930); (Flying Ebony 1925); and (Zev 1923) riding in eight Kentucky Derbies. He had a career record of winning 968 times on 3,673 mounts. He rode from 1918 to 1953 and was elected to the National Thoroughbred Racing Hall of Fame in 1955. He became a trainer after riding and died in 1968[9,10]. **Deceased**

Angel Cordero Jr. – 3 – Cordero, a Puerto Rican won with (Spend A Buck 1985); (Bold Forbes 1976) and (Cannonade 1974) riding in 17 Derbies over a career of 1960 through 1992. He had 7,057 wins riding a total of 38,646 mounts. He received the Eclipse Award as Outstanding Jockey in 1982, 1983 and 1985 and has been elected to the Racing Hall of

Fame. He has given professional advice to other talented jockeys since retiring.[11,12] **Retired**

Gary Lynn Stevens – 3 – Stevens is a mighty fine jockey who has been elected to the National Racing Hall of Fame. He won with (Silver Charm 1997); (Thunder Gulch 1995) and (Winning Colors 1988). These victories and a second on Firing Line in 2015 occurred in eight Derby mounts. From 1979 through 2005 he rode 27,594 mounts with 4,888 wins. He retired briefly but returned to riding in 2013 after serving as a racing analyst for NBC news. He rode primarily on the California circuit.[13,14]
Retired

Kent Jason Desormeaux – 3 – At 19 years he became the all-time holder of the most wins in a single season at 598 in 1989. He has ridden 17 Derby mounts and won on (Big Brown 2008); (Fusaichi Pegasus 2000) and (Real Quiet 1998). His win on Big Brown remains the only horse to ever win the Derby from post position # 20. Twice recipient of the Eclipse Award 1989 and 1992, and Racing Hall of Fame 2004, he received the George Woolf Award for his superb performance as a jockey. He led the nation in the highest number of wins in 1987, 1988, and 1989. Currently riding on the California circuit, he has more than 5,745 wins since he began riding professionally at age 16 years.[15,16] **Active**

Calvin H. Borel – 3 – Borel has ridden on nine Derby mounts and won aboard (Super Saver 2010); (Mine That Bird 2009) and (Street Sense 2007). He retired from racing in 2016 because of injuries, but returned to riding at Ellis Park, Henderson, Kentucky in the same year. Recipient of the Racing Hall of Fame award in 2013, he received the George Woolf Award and the Best Jockey ESPY Award. He has more than 5,146 wins and he currently also rides at Churchill Downs, Fair Grounds and Oaklawn Park.[17,18] **Active.**

Victor Espinosa - 3 His Derby wins include (American Pharoah 2015); (California Chrome 2014); and (War Emblem 2002). He began riding in Mexico and has ridden in the U. S. from 1993 through 2018. He rides the California circuit and has won at least 3,358 riding 21,900 mounts. He received the Best Jockey ESPY Award and the Racing Hall of Fame Award in 2017.[19,20] **Active**

Jerry D. Bailey - 2 - Bailey rode New Discovery in his first Derby in 1982, went on to win twice (Grindstone 1996) and (Sea Hero 1993) and finished 2nd once (Empire Maker 2004) and 3rd once (Blumin Affair 1994) and 4th once (Proper Reality 1988). He had a remarkable 31 – year old career that began in 1974 and ended with his retirement in 2005. He is considered one of the World's All-time Greatest Jockeys and received the Eclipse Award as Outstanding Jockey seven times. He was named to the National Horse Racing Hall of Fame in 1995 and received the George Woolf Memorial Jockey Award in 1992. His record of 30,857 starts shows 5,894 wins, 4,554 seconds and 3,925 thirds.[21,22] **Retired**

Michael Earl Smith – 2 Smith has been successful riding in the Kentucky Derby. His wins include (Justify 2018); (Giacomo 2005); 2nds – 4 - (Bodemeister 2012); (Lion Heart 2004); (Proud Citizen 2002); (Prairie Bayou 1999); 3rd – 1 (Cat Thief 1999). Elected to the National Hall of Fame in 2003, recipient of the George Woolf Memorial Award and Mike Venezia Award for sportsmanship, he began his career in 1982 and continues to ride in the California circuit during 2018. He has had 33,121 mounts with 5,467 wins.[23,24] **Active**

Mario Gutierrez – 2 – Gutierrez is a popular rider based at Santa Anita racetrack. He won the Kentucky Derby aboard (Nyquist 2016); (I'll Have Another 2012), and he has ridden 6,207 mounts with 1,091 wins to date.[25,26] **Active**

John R. Velazquez – 2-wins - He won riding (Always Dreaming 2017); and (Animal Kingdom 2011); second on (Invisible Ink 2001). He received the Eclipse Outstanding Jockey Award in 2004 and 2005, National Hall of Fame 2012, Best Jockey ESPY and George Woolf Memorial Awards. He has 5,000 wins aboard 32,487 mounts.[27,28] **Active**

Other Talented Jockeys

Patrick Alan "Pat" Day – 1 win – (Lil E. Tee 1992); 4 seconds (Menifee 1999); (Forty Niner 1990); (Easy Goer 1989); (Summer Squall 1990); 2 thirds (Prince of Thieves 1996); (Timber Country 1995). Day rode from 1970 through 2008, riding on 48,385 mounts and posted 8,803 victories. He received the Eclipse Outstanding Jockey Award in 1984, 1986, 1987 and 1991. He received the National Racing Hall of Fame Award in 1991, the George Woolf Award and Mike Venezia Award.[29,30] **Retired**

Joel Rosario - 1 win. Born in the Dominican Republic he started riding full time in 2006 in the U. S. He won the Kentucky Derby aboard Orb in 2013. An amazing jockey, he rode 2011 Kentucky Derby winner Animal Kingdom to victory in the USD $6 million Dubai World Cup. He has 2,601 wins in 14, 339 starts.[31,32] **Active**

Robby Albarado - He has ridden from 1990 through 2018 and finished 2nd (Golden Soul 2013) and 3rd twice (Curlin 2007) and (Steppenwolfer 2006) in the Kentucky Derby. He has won 5,136 times with

32,748 mounts.[33,34] **Active**

Jose Lezcano – In a single Derby mount, he finished 2nd. (Ice Box 2010). Lezcano has 2,438 wins on 14,279 mounts.[35,36] **Active**

Javier Castellano – Castellano, born in Venezuela, finished 3rd once (Audible 2018) in the Kentucky Derby. Received the Eclipse Outstanding Jockey Award four times, 2013-2016, since beginning racing career in the U. S. Elected to the Racing Hall of Fame in 2017, he has won 4,924 races aboard 27,078 mounts.[37,38] **Active**

Flavien Prat - Born in Melun, France, he began riding full time in the U. S. In 2015. The son of a trainer, he rode long shot Solomini to 10th position in 2018 Derby and Battle of Midway to 3rd in the 2017 Derby.[39,40] **Active**

Jose L. Ortiz – Ortiz finished 2nd aboard Good Magic in the 2018 Derby and 6th on Tapwrit in 2017. He began riding in the U.S 2012 through 2018 and has 1,568 wins on 8,503 mounts. He received the Eclipse Outstanding Jockey Award in 2017.[41,42] **Active**

Irad Ortiz Jr.- Older brother of Jose this Puerto Rican began riding in the U.S in 2011. He has ridden in the Kentucky Derby aboard these long shots Hofburg 2018 that finished 7th; 2016 My Man Sam 11th and 2014 Uncle Sigh 14th. He received the Shoemaker Award for outstanding riding in 2018.[43,44] **Active**

Shaun Bridgmohan - He finished second aboard Commanding Curve in the 2014 Kentucky Derby. Born in Jamaica, he started riding full time in 1997 in the U. S. He won the Eclipse Award as the Outstanding Apprentice Jockey in 1998 and rides in the New Orleans, Louisville and New York circuits.[45,46]**Active**

Julien Leparoux - He received the Eclipse Apprentice Award and the Outstanding Jockey Award in 2006 after coming to the U.S from France. He has ridden in the Kentucky Derby and finished as follows: 2017 Classic Empire 4th; 2016 Oscar Performance 17th; 2015 Danzig Moon 5th; and 2012 Union Rags. 7th. Classic Empire and Union Rags became outstanding classic winners. He has won 2,274 races to date.[47,48] **Active**

Tyler Gaffalione - He rode Patch to a 14th position in the 2017 Kentucky Derby. This one-eyed colt broke from the 20th position and had little chance of winning. Gaffalione, a Floridian, is the son of a former jockey and grandson of a former jockey. He won his first race in 2014 and later tied Jerry Bailey's 19 - year record by winning seven races on the same day. In 2018. He won his 6th riding title at Gulfstream Park at age 23 years.[49,59] **Active**

Jockey Standings End of Year December 31, 2018[51]

Rank by Name	Starts	Wins	Win %	WPS%
1. Irad Ortiz Jr	1,616	346	21	54
2. Jose L Ortiz	1,513	264	17	48
3. Javier Castellano	1,020	207	20	53
4. Joel Rosario	916	160	17	50
5. Florent Geroux	959	179	19	47
6. John R. Velazquez	823	161	20	45
7. Manuel Franco	1,419	251	20	49
8. Luis Saez	1,465	245	17	49
9. Ricardo Santana Jr	1,075	189	17	46
10. Flavien Prat	829	182	18	46

1. Robby Albarado. 2. Jerry Bailey. 3. Calvin Borel. 4. Javier Castellano. 5. Pat Day. 6. Kent J. Desormeaux. 7. Tyler Gaffalione. 8. Victor Espinosa. 9. Mario Gutierrez. 10. Julien Leparoux. 11. Jose Ortiz. 12. Irad Ortiz Jr. 13. Flavien Prat. 14. Joel Rosario. 15. Michael Smith. 16. Gary Stevens. 17. John R. Velazquez.

CHAPTER 11

HOW TO INTERPRET RACING STATISTICS

Racing Distances

Horse races are run at different distances. The British term "furlong" is a measurement of distance. It is equal to 660 feet, 220 yards, 40 rods, 10 chains and $1/8^{th}$ of a mile. Most races are run at the following distances because some horses perform at their best at a specific distance. Two-year olds race at shorter distances early in their careers and are trained to race at longer distances as they age.

2 furlongs - 1/4 mile	5 furlongs - 5/8 mile
4 furlongs - 1/2 mile	7 furlongs - 7/8 mile
6 furlongs - 3/4 mile	10 furlongs - 1-1/4 mile
8 furlongs - I mile	12 furlongs - 1-1/2 mile

Types of Races

Maiden – The horse has not won a race. Maiden Special Weight is for a horse of top quality, but has not won a race. Maiden Claiming is for a horse of less quality and can be bought "claimed" from the race.

Claiming – The horse is the lowest quality at the track. It can be bought "claimed" for a price. The person must place a request before the race is run. He becomes the owner of the horse, dead or alive. The original owner gets the purse money, not the person who put in the claim and bought the horse.

Allowance - The horse is not for sale or claimed. The winning owner receives more money than in a claiming race. If an allowance horse has raced, but hasn't won for some time, it is allowed to race with 5 lbs less than more successful winners.

Starter Handicaps and Starter Allowances -Horses have started for a certain claiming price since a specific date. The claiming price is listed and the amount the horse has started for at one time to qualify for the race. A Starter Allowance identifies the weight allowance for horses must meet under certain conditions. A Starter Handicap has the weight assigned by the Track Handicapper or Racing Secretary.

Stakes The type of race in which the owner of each horse pays at least part of the money into the total amount raced for. This money is referred to as the entry fee. The final amount is distributed to the finishers as follows: winner 60%, second place 30% and third place 10%. In some instances, the remaining finishers receive a percentage from the total pool. Stakes horses have the highest qualifying credentials.

Dosage Index (Stamina versus Speed)[1]

Many bettors who handicap races use this Index to determine a horse's ability, or inability, to perform at various distances at which a race is run. Dosage means the frequency of a sire to transmit speed or stamina. Some racehorse breeders use it to decide about breeding for speed or for stamina.

For betting purposes, the Index is calculated based on an analysis of the horse's pedigree.[2] The value of 4.00 might be considered as a cut point for judging whether a horse has inherited characteristics for speed or for competing at longer distances. Horses with an Index of 4.00 or more race are considered to race faster in short races. Those with 4.00 or less are considered to perform better at longer distances.

Since the distance of the Kentucky Derby is 1-1/4 miles, owners want a horse capable of racing that distance. They hope to choose one with an Index score of less than 4.00

The index relies on the presence of certain characteristics in the first four generations of a horse's pedigree based on the distances the sires excelled. The **Master List** developed in the 1980s included 120 sires. In April 2005, 85 more have been designated. They have been rated in the **Master List** as follows:

<u>Dosage Profile</u> as:
    Brilliant (Sire's offspring best at short distance),
    Intermediate,
    Classic,
    Solid or
    Professional, (Sire's offspring best at long distance)

If a sire is placed in two different categories, in no case can the categories be more than two positions apart.

If a horse's sire is on the Master List, it counts 16 points for the category to which the sire belongs (or eight in each of two categories if the sire was placed in two groups). a grandsire counts eight points, a great-grandsire four, and a great-great-grandsire two (female progenitors do not count directly, but if any of their sires etc. are on the Master list points would accrue via such sires).

Consider this example: The Dosage Profile 20-14-7-9-0. The Index is determined by adding the first two figures plus one-half the value of the third figure. This figure is divided by one-half of the third figure plus the sum of the last two figures. In this case, it would be 37.5 (20 + 14+ 3.5) divided by 12.5 (3.5 + 9 + 0), giving the horse a Dosage Index of exactly 3.00.

Center of Distribution,

The number of Brilliant points is doubled and added to the number of Intermediate points to obtain the Center of Distribution. This total is subtracted from the number of Solid points and twice the number of Professional points. This number is divided by the total number of points in the entire profile. For example, this would be 54 (40 + 14) minus 9 (9 + 0) divided by 50 (20 + 14 + 7 + 9 + 0), giving a Center of Distribution of 0.8 plus

Horses with high Dosage Index plus Center of Distribution values tend to perform best over shorter distances, while those with low numbers show a preference for longer distances. For North American thoroughbreds, the median Dosage Index is estimated at 2.40 and the average Center of Distribution is 0.70.

Early on, statistical analysis revealed that no horse having a Dosage Index of higher than 4.00 had won the Kentucky Derby since at least 1929.[3,4] Few horses with no master influences in the two most stamina-laden groups, Solid and Professional, had won major races at distances of 1¼ miles or longer even if the horse had a sufficient Classic presence in its pedigree to keep the Dosage Index from being over 4.00.

In recent years, several horses with no Solid or Professional categories in the first four generations of their pedigrees and later won the longer Belmont Stakes with Dosage Indexes of above 4.00. For example, 1999 Kentucky Derby winner Real Quiet had a Dosage Index of 6.02 and 2005 Kentucky Derby winner Giacomo had a Dosage Index of 4.33 but no Solid or Professional points in his Dosage Profile.

Based on outcome of the Kentucky Derby, some handicappers have questioned whether the Index is useful for predicting the winner.[5] Others argue that a number of horses bred in the U. S. with low dosage values have raced in foreign countries at longer distances, resulting in most horses competing in the Derby and similar American races having relatively high Dosage numbers and/or lacking Solid or Professional values. Still, statistical analysis tends to support that the Dosage Index differentiates Thoroughbred pedigree type in large populations of horses engaging in competitive races.

The Blood Horse racing magazine featured details of the Dosage Index in 2009.[6] These figures were listed for each of the entrants in the May 2018 Kentucky Derby edition. Justify, the winner had a 3.0 Index. Good Magic that finished 2nd had 3.40 and 3rd placed finisher Audible had 5.0.

Seven other beaten horses had dosages of 3.00 or less.

Number of Starters Produced by Kentucky Derby Sires, 1875-2018

In the list below, Tapit, Curlin, Tiznow and Malibu Moon are living and still might sire additional starters. A. P. Indy was pensioned in 2011 so his offspring have raced in their last Derby. The others have been deceased long ago. Most of the sires with the highest number of starters stood study duty in Kentucky. They likely sired the most starters because the farms where they stood were close to Churchill Downs.

16 – Black Toney

15 – Enquirer

14 – Broomstick

13 – Sir Gallahad III

12 – Longfellow

11 - A. P. Indy

10 – Ballot; Falsetto, North State III

9 - TAPIT, Heliopolis

8 – CURLIN, Giant's Causeway. Nasrullah, Sweep, The Porter, Budk-den, McGee,

7 – TIZNOW, MALIBU MOON. The others are deceased: Blue Larkspur, Bull Dog, Chicle, Cox's Ridge, Distorted Humor, Fair Play. Hail to Reason, Jim Gaffney, Man o' War, Mr. Prospector, Nashua, Scat Daddy, Tom Broeck.

True Nicks

This is an interesting new system of judging probable success in racing thoroughbreds. Recent evidence shows that the coefficient for breeding and relatedness extends to 10 generations.[7] However, it might be too early to determine its use for wagering on a specific horse. More opportunities may develop once more ratings are assigned to new offspring. Presently, its value is useful for breeding purposes.

True Nicks is a letter rating system dealing with probable success in racing. The score shows the degree of affinity between the sire and broodmare sire, or sire line and broodmare sire line (TrueNicks.com). The rating scale ranges as follows:

A ++	A+	A	B+	B	C+	C	D	F
6.50		4.50	2.50	2.00	1.50	1.25	0.75	0.01	0.00

Horses having an A rating have a higher probability of achieving success than horses with a D rating. The scale has been used to prove matings of stakes-raced horses have been more successful winning than horses of the general horse population. Comparison showed 37% of stakes winners had an A to A++ rating, but just 13% of the general population. Seventy-seven % of stakes winners had a B or better rating compared with 30% the general population. Eight% of 25 stakes winners had C through F ratings while 44% of the general population scored the lowest.

To attain a rating, one must determine SII and BSII numbers. SII is done by comparing the percentage of stakes winners to starters sired by a sire/sire line and out of all mares by a broodmare sire/sire line with the percentage of stakes winners sired by the same sire. An SII of 2.0 means the sire (or sire line) has twice the percentage of stakes winners out of mares by the broodmare sire/sire line as he does when bred to all other mares.

An BSII is done by comparing the percentage of stakes winners to starters by a sire/sire line out of all mares by a broodmare sire/sire line, with the percentage of stakes winners produced by those mares when bred to all other stallions. A value of 3.0 means that the percentage of stakes winners out of mares by the broodmare sire/sire line when bred to the chosen sire/sire line is 3.0 times as high as the percentage of stakes winners produced bt that group of mares when bred to all other stallions.

The True Nicks rating is calculated by multiplying the SII of 2.0 by the 3.0 of BSII. The rating of 6.0 becomes A++.

The information of this system could lead to a better understanding of managing the health of our older sires and dams.

CHAPTER 12

RACE HORSE SELECTIONS

The selection of a horse in the race can be improved by evaluating its racing and training record. By comparing its record to records of other entrants, one can use the information to decide about making a bet. An easy way to start is to examine the workout schedule listed in the chart.[1] It usually reveals the most recent details of the horse's current activity.

Record Description - (Left-Right): Jockey's 2018 Riding Record; Date-Track; Distance-Time; Race Type; Pace; Speed; Post Position; Start-Finish; Jockey; Odds; Top Finisher; Comment; Number of Entrants; Workout Schedule; and Time (Below).

Symbols and Terms[2]

The Jockey's name and record (numbers after the name mean the number of times he has ridden at the track; the number of wins, places and shows).

Trainer's name (numbers after the name mean the number of times he has had a horse race at the track; the number of wins, places and shows)

Race type (Class)- A-allowance; C- claiming; S-stakes

Pars – The average speed rating for a given race.[3] The higher the number, the better the horse is expected to perform.

E – The horse wants to be early on the lead.

E1 – The speed of the horse from the start to the first call (Pace rating)

E2 – The speed of the horse from the start to the second call.

P – The horse wants to press the leader.

E/P – Early Presser is a horse that presses the leader just after leaving the gate.

Numbers 1-8 are points that mean the following: Number 1 is a horse that never wants the lead. The number 8 is a horse that always makes the lead.

Prime Power – A number that is assigned to the horse based on many factors. The higher the number, the better the horse is expected to perform in the race.

Pedigree Rating – The numbers listed for racing on Fast, Wet, Distance and Turf conditions. The higher the number for each, the better is the expectation for performing well.

Pace - how fast a horse runs at different points in a race.

Speed - how fast the horse runs the entire race.

Form - current condition of the horse.

Class - level of competition horse competed against.

Logic favors that the faster the workout time the better the fitness to race. Trainers tend to work quality horses at certain distances Horses are typically galloped 2 miles or less and then their effort may be extended and timed. The effort is usually rated either as **Breezing**, or as **Handily**. Breezing means that the horse is running easily under a hold without encouragement of the rider. Handily means a more strenuous effort where the rider urges the horse, but does not use a whip. Timing of these workouts varies depending on the decision made by the trainer. Most are completed either at 3/8th of a mile, four, or five furlongs. Some horses of higher quality may be timed at either six, seven or eight furlongs.

The record in the chart above shows that this horse has been worked in training every other week.[1] Generally speaking, if a horse races more than once in a month, workouts are omitted. The May 7 record at Churchill Downs of 5 furlongs in 1:00.1 shows that the horse worked 7th out of 23 horses working that distance on the same day.

The Prime Power rating of 142.4 can be compared with Prime Power rating of other horses in the race. The higher the number, the better the performance expected.

The final speed number of 97 of the horse above occurred on May 1, at the Pimlico Race Course. The higher the number, the faster he ran on that day. It exceeded the number that occurred in the previous race on April 14. He finished third, 3/4th of a length behind the leader. Final speed numbers can be compared between any number of horses in the race.

Beyer Speed Figures - In 1973, Andrew Beyer introduced the system of numbers that included the time of the race and inherent speed of the track over which a horse raced.[3] He assigned values in a scale form as follows: 115 - Best; 110 - Good; 90 - Typical $25,000; Typical - 80 - $10,000; and 57 - Bottom Level - $2,000. Horses ranked the highest are expected to produce the best performance. These numbers are available for judging the top speed of a horse in a given race.[4]

Derek Simon discussed the meaning of top speed figures (Beyer speed numbers) in the article titled "It's Time to Call Beyer Speed Figures What They Really Are?[5] He concludes that these figures do not necessarily measure ability. In other words, when a horse races to a higher speed number, it's just part of the happening at that time. The figures are impressive but are not reliable enough to improve one's chance of winning.

In the article "What Do all Triple Crown Winners Have in Common", U. S Racing, March 14, 2017, Derek Simon supports the idea that history shows horses favoring early speed perform well in Triple Crown races.[6] Fans should keep this idea in mind when they evaluate the horse's past races in its racing record.

Considering the recent past history of winners in the Kentucky Derby, Pedigree Consultant, Anne Peters writing in the Blood Horse describes that a history of stamina plays a vital part in the success of winning horses.[7]

She cites that eight of the past 11 winners have been sired by stallions that could win at more than a mile.

In summary, based on the historical importance of both speed and stamina, fans should select horses that show early speed and have been bred by sires with potential for longer distance. If you little to nothing about each, consult with racing analysts who have the experience to advise you.

CHAPTER 13

WAGERING, TYPES OF BETS

Betting on horses is easy, but managing the bet can be tricky. There are many different ways to bet. Pari-mutuel is a French term that means "mutual stake."

Wagering is done via the pari-mutual system where each player is betting against other players, not against the track. Track operations take a certain percentage (cut) from the total pool of dollars wagered. The amount is usually 15 or 20%. The remaining amount is paid to holders of winning tickets.

The $2 wager per horse has been the standard amount for many years.

Straight Bet - $2/horse

Across the Board - an amount that can be bet to win, place and show on the same horse. For example, a $2 bet to win, $2 to place (second), and $2 to show (third) bet on the same horse equals $6.

Daily Double - An amount bet to win on horses in two consecutive races. For example, races 1 and 2 or races 9 and 10.

Pick Three, Four, Five, Six - A bet picking the winner in each of races from three to six groups.

In recent years, **Exotic Betting** has opened new opportunities to wager. The better places a wager on more than one outcome. It offers one of the most profitable way to win larger amounts of money. The amount of money to be bet can range from 10 cents, 50 cents, $1 and up depending on the type of race. Some tracks schedule certain races so that fans can make bets for 10 and 50 cents and others do not.

Exacta – a bet that two horses will finish first and second in the correct order. Example: horses 1 (first) and 5 (second).

Trifecta – a bet in which three horses will finish first, second and 3rd in the correct order. Example: horses 1 (first), 5 (second) and 7 (third).

Superfecta – a bet that the first four horses finish a race in the correct order. Example: horses 1 (first), 5 (second), 7 (third) and 9 (fourth).

Box – a bet that allows for all possible combinations of horses selected, such as Exacta, Trifecta and Superfecta.

Wheel – a bet that includes all combinations to finish in any given order.

Partial Wheel – one horse selected to finish first in a specific position and some of the other horses to finish in the remaining positions that qualify. Example of Trifecta box: # 6 to win, second and third is a tossup between #'s 4, 1 & 8. The possible combinations are 6-4-1-8; 6-1-8; 6-4-1; 6-4-8; 6-8-1; 6-8-4 at a cost of $12.

Full Wheel – Example Trifecta: # 6-All.

Advance Deposit Wagering (ADW)

This kind of betting allows fans to bet over the phone, through the internet or at an OffTrack Betting (OTB) pallor. Churchill downs is one of the states that permits simulcast wagering.[1] There are differences in the manner the betting is handled by the ADW website. Contact one of the websites below for specific details. To sign up, you need to provide your name, address, credit card details and Social Security Number (SSN). The SSN is needed because the IRS requires it. **Websites** Twin Spires, TVG Bet America, Express Bet, and others.

Future Wagering at Churchill Downs

Fans can bet on any probable starter prior to the Kentucky Derby. An article published in the Blood Horse by Frank Angst describes how this can be done. Churchill Downs holds three types of future wagers prior to the race. The pool for each race is run for four days. Odds are listed for each horse on opening day and as the fans bet the odds change through the final day. In past year, the following future wagers have been conducted in November and February,

First Future Wager, Nov. 19, 2018. Bets can be placed on any single nominee or a single bet can be placed on all of the horses. Fans must choose the horse they think can win. These were some of the lowest final odds for the Field (All Horses) and some of the single horses: Field (All horses) - 6/5; Game Winner - 5/1; Coliseum 10/1; Instagram 10/l and Improbable 17/1.

Sire Wager, Nov. 19, : 2019. This bet must select the sire of the winning Derby horse. Here are the final lowest odds for some of the single sires: Tapit - 6/1; Candy Ride - 7/1; Into Mischief 7/1; Curlin 13/1; and All Others 9/2.

Second Future Wager, Feb. 8, 2019 The same type of betting is as in the First Future Wager. Here are the lowest final odds: All Others 5/1; Game Winner - 6/1; Improbable - 8/1; Hidden Schroll - 12/1 and Mucho Gusto - 15/1.

Third Future Wager - March 29, 2019

Fourth Future Wager - April 6, 2019.

On February. 12, Steve Haskins, noted racing analyst, reported his selections of the most likely leading horses as: 1. Game Winner; 2. Improbable; 3. War of Will; 4. Signalman; 5. Win Win Win; 56. Omaha Beach; 7. Nolo Contesto; 8. Mucho Gusto; 9. Hidden Schroll; 10. Global Campaign; 11. Dream Maker; and 12. Bourbon War.

Kentucky Derby Qualifying Point System

A number of prep races are run prior to the Kentucky Derby. Qualifying points are assigned to each race. The number of points varies depending on the quality of horses entered in the race. Quality is determined from the racing record of performance and the amount of money earned by each of the horses entered.

Prior to the Derby, prep races are assigned a specific number of points. Points are awarded to the highest four finishers in each race. The first finisher is ranked with the highest points and the fourth-finisher the least points. The ranking of points for each of the top finishing positions are scored as follows:

100 – 20 -2

50 – 20 - 10

30 – 12 – 6 -1

20 - 8 – 4 - 2

10 – 4 – 2 – 1

The 20 horses with the most points qualify to start in the race.

From September 16, 2017 to April 14, 2018, 45 races conducted across the world received sufficient importance to qualify as prep races. These are:

- United States – 34

    Iroquois Stakes – Churchill Downs

    Front Runner – Santa Anita Park

    Champagne Stakes– Belmont Park

    Breeder's Futurity - Keeneland

    Breeder's Cup Juvenile – Del Mar

    Kentucky Jockey Club – Churchill Downs;

    Remsen – Aqueduct

    Los Alamitos – Los Alamitos Race Course

    Springboard Mile – Remington Park

    Sham Stakes - Santa Anita Park

    Jerome Stakes– Aqueduct

    Le Comte - Fair Grounds;

    Smarty Jones - Oaklawn Park

    Robert B. Lewis – Santa Anita Park

    Withers Stakes - Aqueduct

    Holy Bull – Gulfstream Park

Sam F. Davis – Tampa Bay Downs

El Camino Real Derby – Golden Gate Fields

Risen Star – Fair Grounds

Southwest Stakes – Oaklawn Park

Fountain of Youth – Gulfstream Park

Gotham Stakes – Aqueduct

San Felipe – Santa Anita Park

Tampa Bay Derby – Tampa Bay Downs

Rebel Stakes – Oaklawn Park

Jeff Ruby Stakes – Turfway Park

Louisiana Derby – Fair Grounds

Sunland Derby - Sunland Park

Florida Derby – Gulfstream Park

Wood Memorial – Aqueduct

Blue Grass Stakes – Keeneland

Santa Anita Derby – Santa Anita Park

Arkansas Derby – Oaklawn Park

Lexington Stakes – Keeneland

- ❖ Europe – 7

    Juddmonte Beresford – Naas

    Juddmonte – Newmarket

    Qatar Prix Jean-Luc Legardere - Racing Post Trophy

    Road to the Kentucky Derby Condition Stakes – Kempton Park;

    Patton (Listed) – Dundalk

    Burradon - Newcastle

- ❖ Japan - 3

    Cattier Sho - Tokyo Racecourse

    Zen-Nippon Nisai Yushun – Tokyo Racecourse

    Hyacinth – Tokyo Racecourse

- ❖ Saudi Arabia – 1

    UAE Derby – Meydan Racecourse

These are the final points for the top 10 of the 20 horses that started in the 2018 Kentucky Derby:

Magnum Moon 150

Good Magic 134

Audible 110

Noble Indy 115

Vino Rosso 107

Bolt d'Oro 104

Enticed 103

Mendelsson 100

Justify 100

Quip 90

The interested fan can examine these results and compare them with the outcome of the 2018 Kentucky Derby. Justify won the race, Good Magic finished second and Audible third. All others with higher or lower points finished behind the top three finishers.

In the 2019 March issue of the Blood Horse Daily, Frank Angst updated the points standing for the top 20 horses. The numbers for the top are: Will of War 60; Code of Honor 54; Game Winner 30; Bourbon War 21; Country House 20; Knicks Go 18; Signalman 18; Gunmetal Gray 18; Long Range Teddy 15; Mucho Gusto 14; Tax 12; Mind Control 10; Improbable 10; Harvey Wallbanger 10; Well Defined 10; Vekoma 10; Gray Attempt 10; Anothertwistafate 10; Roildand10; and Hog Creek Hustle 9. Because there are more qualified races to occur, the totals for each horse would increase if it finished higher in other qualified races.

CHAPTER 14

YOU BE THE JUDGE

Opinions are the spice of life. Trying to resolve differences in opinion are fun for some individuals, but miserable for others. Making decisions about winners of the Kentucky Derby offer no exception. For example, should the so-called most famous winners be identified by the fastest speed racing over the track, the margin of victory, problem encountered in race, post time favorite, post position, or condition of racing surface.

A major concern exists in selecting the all-time "best" of all winning horses. Since the selection is the horse, then the choice should be judged entirely on performance by the horse on that Derby day and not other dates prior to or after. In most cases, handicappers and racing writers select from the overall racing record of the horse.

Sometimes, the selection of the best horse overshadows the overall outcome and performance of the event. Relying on published stories need to be evaluated to make comparisons acceptable. Therefore, fans need to evaluate the performance by comparing mathematical data for each horse on racing day.

On the other hand, as a fan of the event, you may wish to decide which Derby race produced the most exciting, provocative, and memorable finish.

First, let's consider some earlier choices of the best horse. Four writers have listed their choices of the best horses as follows:

Prominent racing analyst Andrew Beyer, gave his choices for the best horses in the Washington Post article on May 2, 2017 "The Best Kentucky Derby Winners of All Time."[1] His selections are:

War Admiral 1937 - 2:03.1/5; fast track

Whirlaway 1941 - 2:01.2/5; fast track

Count Fleet 1942 - 2:04 flat; fast track

Citation 1948 - 2.05.2/5, sloppy track

Swaps 1955 – 2:01.4/5, fast track

Majestic Prince - 1969 – 2:01.4/5, fast track

Secretariat - 1973 - 1:59.2/5, fast track

Seattle Slew - 1977 - 2:02.1/5, fast track

Affirmed - 1978 - 2:01.1/5, fast track

Spectacular Bid, 1979 – 2:02.2/5 fast track

Spend a Buck - 1985 – 2:00.1/5 fast track

Alysheba - 1987 – 2:03 flat, fast track

Sunday Silence - 1989 – 2:05 flat, fast track

Silver Charm - 1997 – 2:02.2/5, fast track

Beyer did not distinguish one horse as better than the others on the list. He did not select entirely by race time. However, a look at the list based on race time is interesting. Secretariat ran the fastest and Spend a Buck, Affirmed and Whirlaway followed. Citation raced slowest, likely due to the wet track condition. Since seven winners he selected went on to capture the Triple Crown, Beyer may have chosen partly on the complete race record of each horse.

In Louisville Life, a Louisville magazine, 2017, Brandon Quick listed "The Top 10 Derby Winners of All Time."[2] He ranked these in order:

10. Gallant Fox - 1930 - 2:07.3/5; good

9. Whirlaway - 1941 - 2:01.2/5; fast

8. Count Fleet - 1943 - 2:04 flat; fast

7. Northern Dancer - 1964; 2:00 flat; fast

6. Barbaro - 2006 - 2:01.36; fast

5. American Pharoah - 2015; 2:03.02; fast

4. Seattle Slew -1971 - 2:02.1/5; fast

3. Citation -1948 - 2:05.2/5; sloppy

2. Spectacular Bid -1979 - 2:02.2/5; fast

1. Secretariat 1973 - 1:59.27; fast

Secretariat wins over the others on time. Northern Dancer's time is better than the remainder on the list. For other Derby winners not listed, the time by 2001 winner Monarchos surpasses the remainder after Secretariat. None of the other nine ran faster than Decidedly, Proud Clarion, Grindstone or Fusaichi Pegasus. Slight latitude can be allowed for the performance of Gallant Fox. He raced on a track rated as good when he beat Gallant Knight by two lengths. He would have been soundly defeated by Smarty Jones and by Citation as both raced on a sloppy track. Smarty Jones beat Lion Heart by 2 1/2 lengths and Citation won easily by 3 1/2 lengths over stable mate Coaltown.

Any interpretation based on post position is open to question (See post position, Chapter 10). Some horses raced in smaller fields than others. Less crowding for position and bumping would occur in smaller fields opposite of the 2018 Derby with 20 entrants. For example, Citation ran from position 1 against five other horses; Johnstown, post 5 against 6 others; Gallahadion, post 1 and Majestic Prince, post 8, each against 7 others; Iron Liege ran from post 6 and Chateaugay from post 1, each against 8 others.

In Southern Living magazine, Caroline Rogers listed the following horses in the 2018 article "These Are the Most Famous Horses from Kentucky Derby History."[3]

Donerail 1913 - 2:04.4/5; fast track

Seattle Slew 1977 - 2:02.1/5; fast track

Secretariat 1973 - 1:59.2/5; fast track

Spectacular Bid 1977 - 2:02.2/5; fast track

Affirmed 1978 - 2:01.1/5; fast track

Genuine Risk - 1980 - 2:02 flat; fast track

Monarchos - 2001 - 1:59.97; fast track

Smarty Jones - 2004 - 2:04.06; sloppy track

California Chrome - 2014 - 2:03.66; fast track

American Pharoah - 2015 - 2:03.02; fast track

Nyquist - 2016 - 2:01.31; fast track

Using fastest speed over the track, Secretariat and Monarchos easily surpassed all others. By comparison with other winners, Northern Dancer – (2:00 flat; fast), Spend A Buck (2:00.1/5; fast), Decidedly (2:00. 1/5; fast), Proud Clarion (2:00.3/5; fast), Grindstone (2:01 flat; fast) and Fusaichi Pegasus (2:01: flat; fast) bested the rest.

Using margin of victory, four horses won by 8 lengths, Old Rosebud (1914 2:03.2/5 - fast); Johnstown (1939 2:03.2/5 - fast); Whirlaway (1941 2:01.2/5 - fast); Assault (1946 2:06.3/5 - slow) and two Barbaro (2006 2:01.36 - fast) and Mine That Bird (2009 2:02.66 – fast)) won by 6 ½ lengths. These names are missing from the list above.

In the 2018 report "Run for The Roses: 8 Most Famous Winners of The Kentucky Derby" Nina Lin[4] of NBC chose the following:

Aristides 1785 - race I-1/2 half mile - 2:37.3/4; fast

Iron Liege 1957 - 2:01.1/5; fast

Seattle Slew 1971 - 2:02.1/5; fast

Secretariat 1973 - 1:59.27; fast

Affirmed 1978 - 2:01.1/5; fast

Barbaro 2006 - 2;01.36; fast

Mine That Bird, 2009 - 2:02.36; fast

American Pharoah 2015 - 2:03.02; fast

Secretariat wins easily over all others. Iron Liege and Barbaro times are faster and margin of victory is greater than the remainder. However, Barbaro's time and those of the others are slower than the times recorded by Northern Dancer, Decidedly, Proud Clarion, Grindstone and Fusaichi Pegasus.

Spokane's record, 1889; 2:34.1-1/2; fast track smashed Aristides 1885 time over the fast track.

While the opinions rendered in the four articles (above) are interesting, perhaps more intriguing would be the Derby races chosen by closeness of finish or when complications affected the outcome and not the selection of best horses. For example, the most exciting races might be any the following:

 Dark Star-Native Dancer 1953

 Iron Liege-Gallant Man 1957

 Tomy Lee-Sword Dancer 1959

 Grindstone-Cavonnier 1996

 Dancer's Image-Forward Pass 1968

 Silver Charm-Captain Bodgit 1997

 Broker's Tip-Head Play 1933

 The Dark Star-Native Dancer race finish produced a spectacular outcome. Dark Star broke from post 10 and led all the way. Native Dancer broke from the difficult post position 1 and lost by a head. Various scribes and fans thought Native Dancer lost because Money Broker had severely crossed over on him early in the race at the Clubhouse turn. Eleven horses raced over a fast track with Dark Star timed in 2:02 flat. He became to be the only horse to beat Native Dancer that went on to win 21 of 22 lifetime starts.

 The Tomy Lee-Sword Dancer race gave us more than expected. Willie Shoemaker agreed to ride Tomy Lee before the Derby. He had ridden Sword Dancer to victory in another race the week before. Bill Boland got the mount on Sword Dancer. Driving toward the finish, Tomy Lee had a short lead, but Shoemaker thought he seemed to tire. The two horses bumped several times and Sword Dancer passed Tomy Lee. Shoemaker spoke to Boland "Good luck, I hope you win it." As they closed near the finish, Tomy Lee regained the lead and won by a nose. Boland claimed a foul, but the judges disallowed it.

The Iron Liege-Gallant Man race caught the eye of the press. They attributed the loss by Gallant Man to jockey Willie Shoemaker. Calumet Farm's Iron Liege had the lead heading toward the finish line. Gallant Man began closing and Shoemaker stood up in his irons at the 1/16 marker. Iron Liege won by a nose. When questioned by the judges, he replied that Gallant Man had taken a bad step. Later, he admitted that he had misjudged the 1/16 pole as the finish line. The judges suspended him 15 days for "Gross carelessness."

The Grindstone-Cavonnier finish proved too close to call. This race turned out to be another D. Wayne Lukas-Bob Baffert contest. Grindstone, one of five horses Lukas entered, had a terrible start breaking from an outside post position 15. Cavonnier, a gelding ridden by Chris McCaron and trained by Baffert started from post position 3. As the race began, Jerry Bailey riding Grindstone, saved ground early on with Grindstone running fourth from last. Cavonnier ran in ninth position on the backside and moved to third entering the stretch. Grindstone behind Cavonnier, raced forward on the far turn. Bailey got Grindstone through along the rail at the head of the stretch. Moving toward the finish Cavonnier grabbed a slight lead and looked like he had enough left to win. Near the 1/8 marker, Grindstone had to shift outside of three inside horses to catch Cavonnier. As Cavonnier headed near the finish, Grindstone closed sharply on the outside with a powerful rush under the left-handed whipping by Bailey. He and Cavonnier finished too close to decide the winner at the wire. Both Chris McCarron and Bob Baffert thought Cavonnier had won. But an examination of the finishing photo showed Grindstone the winner by a nose or a lip. The time of 2:01 flat was the seventh fastest time recorded in Derby history.

The Dancer's Image-Forward Pass outcome still leaves some fans, owner, trainer and jockey with a bitter taste. As Peter Fuller's Dancer's Image crossed the finish line, he had beaten Calumet Farm's Forward Pass. However, Fuller's trouble had just begun. Dancer's Image, suffering with arthritis had been administered Phenylbutazone (Bute) earlier in the day. According to Kentucky rules of racing, Bute was not permitted on race day. Fuller and Lou Cavalaris Jr the trainer of Dancer's Image, assumed that the Bute would clear from the horse by post time. It did not. Fuller argued that someone else had given Dancer's Image another dose. The outcome proved sour for Fuller. According to the Kentucky State Racing Commission, the purse money was redistributed with first-place money going to Forward Pass who would be listed as the official winner. Dancer's Image was placed last.

Fuller filed an appeal about the Derby decision. In December 1970, a Kentucky Court awarded first place to Dancer's Image. In 1972, the Kentucky State Court overturned the decision. Fuller claimed that he had been set up because he had donated $62,000 of prize money for a previous victory to Coretta King, widow of Martin Luther King, two days after King's death.

The Silver Charm-Captain Bodgit Derby brought smiles to the face of the winner and tears to the eyes of the loser. The race began with Silver Charm racing from post position number 6 and Captain Bodgit from post position number 5. Silver Charm broke close to the front with Captain Bodgit further behind. Racing around the far turn and into the stretch Silver

Charm closed and gained the lead. Captain Bodgit racing sixth in the stretch closed suddenly on the outside nearing the finish. Silver Charm held on to win by a close neck.

Broker's Tip-Head Play race continues as one of the zaniest outcomes on record. A photographer bent down in the infield snapped a photo of jockey Don Meade riding Broker's Tip and Herb Fisher riding Head Play battling each other nearing the finish. They also fought again in the jockey dressing room after the race. Loser Herb Fisher delivered the first blow.

As the race began, Head Play broke from the starting gate and stayed close to the lead. Owned by Col E. R. Bradley of Idle Hour Farm, Broker's Tip, a maiden, got off slowly because of an outside post position. Head Play had the lead at the top of the stretch with Broker's Tip about three lengths behind in third. Heading toward the finish line, Jockey Fisher noticed Broker's Tip closing near the inner rail. He reached over and grabbed the saddle on Broker's Tip in an attempt to prevent Broker's Tip from passing. Meade grabbed the left sleeve of Fisher's shirt. They fought to the finish. No finish-line photograph was taken in 1933 as is done today. Four judges looking through binoculars decided which horse won.

Three of the judges agreed that Head Play had won, but one overruled them. The victory went to Broker's Tip because the judges agreed again that Fisher interfered with the stride of the fast closing Broker's Tip. The judges interviewed both jockeys and Meade claimed that he would have won by two to three lengths rather than by the nose victory. Thirteen entrants competed and the winner's time of 2:06.4/5 occurred on a track labeled good to muddy.

Both jockeys received a suspension of one month. Meade received three additional lifetime suspensions land never competed as a jockey again. Thirty-two years after the 1933 race, the jockeys met and shook hands.

CHAPTER 15

TRAVEL ARRANGEMENTS TO RACE TRACK

DIRECTIONS [1]

Express Access to 700 Central Avenue, Churchill Downs

Non-Derby and Oaks Days

- Driving from Indianapolis, Downtown Louisville, Points North: I-65 South: Take Exit 132 – Crittenden Drive, continue and take first right at Central Avenue, continue and turn left on Kentucky Derby Drive to enter Churchill Downs.

- Driving from Lexington and Points East: I-64W Lexington, I-264 West): Take Exit 10 – Third St./Southern Pkwy. Turn right heading north on Third St. or Southern Pkwy to Central Ave., continue to Kentucky Derby Drive to enter Churchill Downs.

- Driving from Nashville and Points South: I-65 North or from Airport: Take I-264 West (Watterson Expressway) to Exit 10 - Third St./Southern Pkwy. Turn right heading north on Third St. or Southern

Pkwy to Central Avenue, continue and turn left onto Kentucky Derby Drive to enter Churchill Downs.

- ❖ Driving from St. Louis and Points West: I-264 East (from I-64E – New Albany and St. Louis): Take Exit 9 – Taylor Blvd. Turn left traveling north on Taylor Blvd. Turn right on Central Avenue, continue and turn right onto Kentucky Derby Drive to enter Churchill Downs.

Derby and Oaks Day

Unfortunately, Churchill Downs changed its locations on Non-Derby and Non-Oaks days to reduce traffic flow around the track.[1] Central Avenue located between Crittenden Drive and Taylor Blvd. Is closed to public traffic on Friday, Saturday and restricted on Thursday in the first week of May. Only shuttles and taxis can be driven down Central Avenue during the Kentucky Oaks and Kentucky Derby days. Pedestrians walking toward Churchill Downs must cross on Third and Ninth Streets only. A bus depot, a pedestrian bridge at Central Avenue and a Paddock entrance gate have been added.

LOCAL TRANSPORTATION

Taxi Services - Yellow Cab is the Official Taxicab of Churchill Downs and your ride to and from the racetrack. The Yellow Cab stand is conveniently located on site at Gate 17 for drop offs and pick-ups before and after the races.

Limousine Services - Xtreme Transportation, the preferred Limousine service of Churchill Downs, is one of the largest providers of private and executive transportation in the Louisville, Kentucky/Southern Indiana area. It has a wide range of vehicles to meet the traveler's needs, large and small, from Sedans to SUV's, Vans, Limousines and Buses.
Contact info@xtremetransportation.com for information and pricing, or call directly at (812) 246-2235.

Sentient Jet Services - Travel with Sentient Jet, is the Preferred Private Aviation Partner of Churchill Downs. Sentient Jet has perfected the jet card model. Its Sentient Jet Card program is available for attendees of the Kentucky Derby. See Nike -Sentient Jet Services, 696-654-3445.

CHAPTER 16

ARRIVAL AT TRACK

The property of Churchill Downs is located close to the I-264 Expressway. Entrance to the backside of the track can be reached by exiting to Southern Parkway leading to South 4th Street or to Taylor Boulevard. The backside of the grounds runs along Longfield Avenue. The Clubhouse Gate (Gate 10) opens into a large parking lot. Traveling from downtown, the front entrance can be reached off Central Avenue. The Paddock Gates (Gates 1 and 10) provide easy access to the Grandstand and the Clubhouse.

The space between Gates 1 and 17 is combined to form the Paddock Gate.[1] Fans can access the track through this entrance after buying a General Admission or Reserved ticket. The statue of the 2006 Kentucky Derby winner Barbaro is located in front of the Kentucky Derby Museum and Main gate.

Clubhouse ticket holders must enter through the Clubhouse Gate (Gate 10). Take the path between the First Turn Suites and the blue lot.

General admission ticket holders can also enter the Infield Gate (Gate 3) at the corner of Oakdale Avenue and South 4th Street. The ticket holder must enter through the Infield Gate if they carry a chair.

Gate 12 allows exit to Queen Avenue from the Parking Lot.

All on-site parking on Kentucky Derby and Kentucky Oaks days is reserved.[2] A parking pass is needed. Fans without parking passes can park at Papa John's Cardinal Stadium, the Kentucky Expo Center, or on streets in surrounding neighborhoods if space is available.

GATE CHANGES

Churchill Downs changed the numbered gates to names. Former Gate 3 is now called "Infield Gate." Former Gate 10 is now labeled "Clubhouse Gate." Fans with general admission tickets and those with reserved seats can enter through "Paddock Gate", formerly Gates 1 and 17. Tickets are scanned at kiosks inside the Paddock entrance.

CHAPTER 17

PLACES TO STAY NEARBY

Motels Within Number of Miles of Churchill Downs[1,2]

0.5

- Super 8 Hotel Expo Center, 68 rooms, 101 Central Avenue, Louisville, 40209 – (502) 694-3664

1.1

- Holiday Inn Airport Louisville, 106 rooms, 447 Farmington Avenue, Louisville, 40209 – (502) 637-4500
- Home 2 Suites by Hilton Airport Louisville, 3000 Crittenden Drive, Louisville, 40209 - (502) 916-3800
- Hilton Garden Inn Louisville Airport, 210 rooms, 2735 Crittenden Drive, Louisville, 40209, (502) 637-2424
- Ramada Limited Hotel Airport Louisville, 49 rooms, 2912 Crittenden Drive, Louisville, 40209, (502) 753-5555
- Four Points by Sheraton Hotel Louisville Airport, 117 rooms, 2850 Crittenden Drive, Louisville, 40209, (502) 753-5555

1.3

- Holiday Inn Louisville Airport – Fair/Expo, 447 Farmington Avenue, 40209, (502) 637-4500
- Home 2 Suites by Hilton Louisville Airport/Expo Center, Ky. 2735 Crittenden Drive, 40209, (502) 916-3800
- Super 8 by Wyndham Louisville/Expo Center, 101 Central
- Avenue, 40209, (502) 694-3664
- Four Points by Sheraton Louisville Airport, 2850 Crittenden Drive, 40209, (502) 753-5555
- Ramada by Wyndham Expo Center, 2912 Crittenden Drive 40209, (855) 213-0582

1.6

- Quality Inn & Suites East Gaulbert Louisville, 87 rooms, 311 East Gaulbert Avenue, Louisville, 40208 (502) 638-6100
- Days Inn Louisville, 142 rooms, 1620 Arthur Street, Louisville, 40208 (502) 636-3781
- Rodeway Inn Louisville, 66 rooms, 571 Phillips Lane, Louisville, 40209 (502) 361-5008
- Inn at St. James Court, 1440 St. James Court, 40208 (866) 430-2692

2.0-2.8

- Crowne Plaza Louisville Airport Expo Center, 830 Phillips Lane, 40209 (502) 367-2251
- La Quinta Inn & Suites Louisville Airport & Expo, 4125 Preston Hwy., 40213 (855) 823-4661

3.3-3.7

- Omni Louisville Hotel, 400 South 2nd Street, 40202 (502) 313-6664
- Galt House Hotel, 140 North 4th Street, 1,300 rooms, 40202 (502) 589-5200

PARKING

Parking at Churchill Downs is limited only to guests with reserved parking passes. Fans with reserved parking passes can enter either on Gate 10 on Longfield Avenue or Gate 12 on Queen Avenue Taylor Blvd.

Papa John's Cardinal Stadium: The Stadium is located at 2800 S. Floyd Street. Parking on Kentucky Derby or Kentucky Oaks days costs $20/day. Parking and shuttles are free on Tuesday and Wednesday of Derby week. On Thursday, the parking is still free, but no shuttles are available. Walking to the track takes about 20 minutes.

Kentucky Expo Center: Most other parking options for Kentucky Derby week are offsite at the Kentucky Exposition Center, 937 Phillips Lane. Fans wishing to park on Derby Day or Oaks Day must buy a Churchill Downs admission ticket by the Derby or Oaks day. Parking lots are reserved for ticket holders. The permits sold with tickets include free shuttle to the track.

On Thursday, parking with a shuttle is free. Uber, Lyft and Hotel shuttles drop off and pick up at Papa John's Cardinal Stadium and the Kentucky Expo Center. Parking in nearby neighborhoods still remains if spaces are open.

ACKNOWLEDGMENTS

It's a pleasure to thank my wife Madge who has remained steadfast in her support of this manuscript. She has offered numerous suggestions about the text and has helped in managing the images.

In Virginia, I'd like to express my appreciation to Brenda Gibrall who proofread the manuscript and made significant corrections and arrangements of text material.

In Virginia, I wish to express my gratitude to Mathew Butler who took the time to provide me with the 1946 Kentucky Derby ticket that is shown on the book cover.

Cathy R of the Brad H. Cox Stable was kind to send me the copy of his photo that has contributed greatly to my collection of trainer images.

REFERENCES

CHAPTER 1: KENTUCKY DERBY HOW IT STARTED

1. Kentucky Derby: Churchill Downs History. Wikipedia: The Free Encyclopedia; Wikimedia Foundation, Inc.
2. Dulay, C.P. The Kentucky Derby Is Inarguably the Most Famous and Important Race in North America For 3-year Old Thoroughbreds. Thought Co., April 7, 2018.
3. Churchill Downs: History of Churchill Downs, 2018.
4. Thomas, S.W. Churchill Downs: A Documental History of America's Most Legendary Race Track. Kentucky Derby, 1995.
5. Jennings, Kathleen. The Churchill Family. Chapter V. The Standard Printing Co. Louisville, Ky 1920.
6. Gatto, K. Churchill Downs: America's Most Historic Racetrack. The History Press, Charlestown, S.C. 2010.
7. Demling, Jody. The Annual Grade 1 Stakes Race., "The "Run for the Roses" Has Long Been the Biggest Showcase of American Horse Racing. SportsLine, May 2, 2018.
8. Bolus, Jim. Run for The Roses. 100 Years at The Kentucky Derby. Hawthorn Books, Inc. New York, 1974.

CHAPTER 2: ADMISSION AND SEATING ARRANGEMENT

1. Seating Chart: Kentucky Oaks & Derby Week, Churchill Downs, Inc, 2019.
2. Kentucky Derby Seating Info. Derby Box., www.derbybox.com.

3. Churchill Downs Seating Chart: Kentucky Derby Seating Chart. Tick Pick Blog.

CHAPTER 3: SITES ON THE GROUNDS

1. Historic American Building Survey C; Churchill Downs, 700 Central Avenue Louisville, Jefferson Co, Ky. Library of Congress.
2. Gentry, Lewis. L. Track's Iconic Feature Made It Famous. History of Twin Spires. Designed by Joseph Dominic Baldez, May 7, 2005.

CHAPTER 4: TRACK SERVICES AND FACILITIES

1. Guest Services: Churchill Downs Racetrack: Home of the Kentucky Derby, Churchill Downs Inc. wwwchurcholldowns.com

CHAPTER 5: LOCATING FOOD AND DRINK

1. Friend. Nina. This Is the 2018 Kentucky Derby Menu. www.foodandwine.com, March 28, 2018.
2. Jazzy Morgan. Official 2018 Kentucky Derby R Tickets Breakdown: Turf Club & Roses Lounge: Derby Experiences. October 6, 2017.

CHAPTER 6: DAILY RACING PROGRAMS, TIPS, AND NEWS

1. Dailey Racing Form.
2. Equibase.
3. Brisnet.
4. Horse Racing Nation
5. Blood Horse. com

6. TruNicks, com

7. U.S. Racing News and Handicapping Reports,

8. Paulick Report

CHAPTER 7: FACTORS AFFECTING WINS

1. Foster, S.C. My Old Kentucky Home Good Night, 1953 Library of Congress.

2. Archer, J. D. Rogers Kentucky Derby Fun Facts. Churchill Downs, 137 Derby. Spring 2011.

3. Kentucky Derby Wins by Post Position. newsday.com, May 1, 2018.

4. Demling, Jody. Kentucky Derby Post Positions. America's Best Racing, May 1, 2017.

5. Dulay, Cindy. Pierson. A List of the Kentucky Derby's Fastest Winners. ThoughtCo. April 7, 2018.

6. Petrella, Steve. Kentucky Derby Records and All-time Leaders, Sporting News, May 5, 2018.

7. A Muddy Track in the Kentucky Derby: Is It an excuse? Preakness Field and Analysis. The Washington Post 2013.

8. West, Jenna. Justify Breaks the "Apollo. Curse" With Kentucky Derby Win. Sports Illustrated, May 5, 2018.

9. Latex Found to Bip Horse's Performance Racing. A Study Also Found That the Drug Used to Control Bleeding Does Not Always Work. Los Angeles Times, May 7, 1990.

10. Demling, Jody. 10 Years Ago: Eight Belles Shocking Breakdown at Kentucky Derby. Louisville Courier Journal, May 5, 2018.

CHAPTER 8: FAMOUS OWNERS

1. Horse Racing Nation. Com
2. Bower, Alex. Derby Wins of Triple Crown Victors; Citation. Blood Horse, April 25, 2017.
3. Calumet Farm. Wikipedia: The Free Encyclopedia. Wikimedia Foundation, Inc.
4. E.R. Bradley. National Museum of Horse Racing. Saratoga Springs, New York, 2014.;
5. E. R. Bradley. Wikipedia: The Free Encyclopedia: Wikimedia Foundation, Inc.
6. Belair Stud. The Vault: Horseracing Present and Past thevaultwordpress.com.
7. Belair Stud. Wikipedia: The Free Encyclopedia: Wikimedia Foundation, Inc.
8. Bashford Manor Stable. Wikipedia: The Free Encyclopedia. Wikimedia Foundation, Inc.
9. Harry Payne Whitney. Like Father: Like Son. americasracing.net.
10. Harry Payne Whitney. Wikipedia: The Free Encyclopedia: Wikimedia Foundation, Inc.
11. The Hertz Foundation. John Daniel Hertz. hertzfoundation.org.
12. John D. Hertz/American Businessman - /britannica.com.
13. Voss, Natalie. Kentucky Farm Time Capsule: Greentree Stud. Paulick Report January 28, 2018.

14. Greentree Stable. Wikipedia: The Free Encyclopedia. Wikimedia Foundation Inc.

15. The King Ranch Legacy kingranch.com.

16. King Ranch: Wikipedia: The Free Encyclopedia. Wikimedia Foundation Inc.

17. Darby Dan Farm - Devoted to The Horse; Dedicated To Our Clients darbydan.com.

18. Darby Dan Farm. Wikipedia: The Free Encyclopedia. Wikimedia Foundation Inc.

19. Christopher Chenery. Wikipedia: The Free Encyclopedia. Wikimedia Foundation Inc.

20. Secretariat's Birthplace At the Meadow Named to Virginia Landmark Register. www.meadowevventpark.com.

21. Bob & Beverly Lewis - Beloved Racing Royalty. www.bloodhorse.com. October 23, 2017.

22. Beverly Lewis Passes Away at Age 90. Horse Racing News: Police Report, October 23, 2017.

23. J. Paul Reddam. Wikipedia: The Free Encyclopedia. Wikimedia Corp. Inc.

24. J. Paul Reddam. Headlines. Blood Horse, p 1 & 3. www.bloodhorse.com.

CHAPTER 9: IDENTIFYING LEADING TRAINERS

1. Ben Jones. Encyclopedia Britannica.

2. Ben Jones Wikipedia: The Free Encyclopedia. Wikimedia Foundation. Inc.

3. Bob Baffert. Trainer Profile – Equibase. Com.

4. Bob Baffert. America's Best Racing.

5. D. Wayne Lukas. - Trainer Profile - D. Wayne Lucas – Equibase. Com.

6. D. Wayne Lukas. Wikipedia: The Free Encyclopedia. Wikimedia Foundation, Inc.

7. H. J. Thompson. Wikipedia: The Free Encyclopedia. Wikimedia Foundation, Inc.

8. James Fitzsimmons. Wikipedia: The Free Encyclopedia. Wikimedia Foundation, Inc.

9. Max Hirsch. Wikipedia: The Free Encyclopedia. Wikimedia Foundation, Inc.

10. Nick Zito. Wikipedia: The Free Encyclopedia. Wikimedia Foundation, Inc.

11. Trainer Profile - Nick Zito - Equibase. Com

12. Doug O' Neill. Wikipedia: The Free Encyclopedia. Wikimedia Foumdation, Inc.

13. Doug O'Neill. Trainer. Horse Racing Nation.

14. Todd Pletcher. Wikipedia: The Free Encyclopedia. Wikimedia Foundation, Inc.

15. Charles Whittingham. Encyclopedia Britannica.

16. Woodford P. Stephens. - Trainer Profile. Equibase. Com

17. Woody Stephens. The Encyclopedia Britannica.

18. LeRoy Jolley. Wikipedia: The Free Encyclopedia. Wikimedia Foundation, Inc.

19. Trainer Profile - Leroy Jolley - Equibase.

20. Laz Barrera. Wikipedia: The Free Encyclopedia. Wikimedia Foundation, Inc.

21. Lucien Laurin. Wikipedia: The Free Encyclopedia. Wikimedia Foundation, Inc.

22. Lucien Laurin. Secretariat. Com.

23. Henry Forest. Wikipedia: The Free Encyclopedia. Wikimedia Foundation, Inc.

24. Henry Forest. 67, Top Horse Trainer. The New York Times.

25. Horatio Luro. Wikipedia: The Free Encyclopedia. Wikimedia Foundation, Inc.

26. Horace A. Jones. Wikipedia: The Free Encyclopedia. Wikimedia Foundation, Inc.

27 Horace A. Jones. The Top 26 Kentucky Derby Trainers. ThoughtCo.

28. Carl Nafzger. Wikipedia: The Free Encyclopedia. Wikimedia Foundation, Inc.

29. Biography. Carl Nafzger. Kentucky Derby Trainers. ThoughtCo.

30. Claude R. McGaughey III. Wikipedia: The Free Encyclopedia. Wikimedia Foundation, Inc.

31. Claude McGaughey III. America's Best Racing.

32. H. Graham Motion. America's Best Racing.

33. Trainer Profile - H, Graham Motion - Equibase.

34. Dale Romans. Wikipedia: The Free Encyclopedia. Wikimedia Foundation, Inc.

35. Roman's Impresses Mott as All-Time Leading Trainer at Historic Churchill Downs. November 12, 2017.

36. Steve Asmussen. Wikipedia: The Free Encyclopedia. Wikimedia Foundation, Inc.

37. Chad C. Brown. Wikipedia: The Free Encyclopedia. Wikimedia Foundation, Inc.

38. J. Larry. Jones. Wikipedia: The Free Encyclopedia. Wikimedia Foundation, Inc.

39. Kenneth McPeek. Wikipedia: The Free Encyclopedia. Wikimedia Foundation, Inc.

40. Trainer Profile - Kenneth G. McPeek - Equibase. com.

41. Ian Wilkes. America's Best Racing.

42. Ian Wilkes. Horse Racing Nation.

43. Mark Casse. America's Best Racing.

44. Mark G. Casse. Wikipedia: The Free Encyclopedia. Wikimedia Foundation, Inc.

45. William I. Mott. National Museum of Horse Racing and Hall of Fame.

46. William I. Mott. Wikipedia: The Free Encyclopedia. Wikimedia Corp. Inc.

47. Michael J. Maker. Wikipedia: The Free Encyclopedia. Wikimedia.Foundation, Inc.

48. Trainer Profile. - Michael J. Maker - Equibase. Com.

49. Brad Cox Racing. Home.

50. Brad H. Cox. America's Best Racing.

51. Leading Trainers in 2018 North America Through December 31. 2018. Equibase. Com.

CHAPTER 10: WINNING AND TALENTED JOCKEYS

1. Eddie Arcaro. Wikipedia: The Free Encyclopedia, Wikimedia Foundation, Inc.
2. Eddie Arcaro. Encyclopedia Britannica.
3. Bill Hardtack-Wikipedia: The Free Encyclopedia, Wikimedia Foundation, Inc.
4. Bill, Christine. The Bittersweet Life of a Hall of Fame Jockey. McFarland & Co. Jefferson, North Carolina 2016
5. William Shoemaker. National Museum of Racing and Hall of Fame.
6. Bill Shoemaker Biography. Encyclopedia of World Biography, 2004.
7. Isaac Murphy. Wikipedia: The Free Encyclopedia. Wikimedia Foundation, Inc.
8. Isaac Burns Murphy. National Museum of Racing and Hall of Fame.
9. Earl Sande. National Museum of Racing and Hall of Fame.
10. Earl Sande. Wikipedia: The Free Encyclopedia. Wikimedia Foundation, Inc.
11. Angel Cordero Jr. Wikipedia: The Free Encyclopedia. Wikimedia Foundation, Inc.
12. Angel Cordero Jr. National Museum of Racing and Hall of Fame.
13. Gary L. Stevens. America's Best Racing.
14. Gary L. Stevens, Equibase. Com.
15. Kent J, Desormeaux. Wikipedia: The Free Encyclopedia. Wikimedia Foundation, Inc.
16. Kent J. Desormeaux. Equibase. Com
17. Calvin Borel. Wikipedia: The Free Encyclopedia. Wikimedia Foundation, Inc.

18. Calvin Borel. Equibase Com
19. Victor Espinosa. Wikipedia: The Free Encyclopedia. Wikimedia Corp. Inc.
20. Victor Espinosa. Equibase. Com.
21. Jerry D. Bailey. Wikipedia: The Free Encyclopedia. Wikimedia Foundation, Inc.
22. Jerry D. Bailey. Equibase, Com.
23. Michael Earl Smith. Wikipedia: The Free Encyclopedia. Wikimedia Foundation, Inc.
24. Michael Smith. Jockey, Horse Racing Nation.
25. Mario Gutierrez (Jockey). Wikipedia: The Free Encyclopedia. Wikimedia Foundation, Inc.
26. Mario Gutierrez. Equibase. Com.
27. Joseph R. Velazquez. Wikipedia: The Free Encyclopedia. Wikimedia Foundation, Inc.
28. John Velazquez, Horse Racing Nation.
29. Pat Day. Wikipedia: The Free Encyclopedia. Wikimedia Foundation, Inc.
30. Pat Day. National Museum of Racing and Hall of Fame.
31. Joel Rosario. Wikipedia: The Free Encyclopedia. Wikimedia Foundation, Inc.
32. Joel Rosario. Equibase. Com.
33. Robby Albarado. America's Best Racing.
34. Robby Albarado. Wikipedia: The Free Encyclopedia. Wikimedia Foundation, Inc.

35. Jose Lezcano. Wikipedia: The Free Encyclopedia. Wikimedia Foundation, Inc.
36. Jose Lezcano (Jockey). Horse Racing News.
37. Javier Castellano. Wikipedia: The Free Encyclopedia. Wikimedia Foundation, Inc.
38. Javier Castellano. America's Best Racing.
39. Flavien Prat. America's Best Racing.
40. Flavien Prat. Wikipedia: The Free Encyclopedia. Wikimedia Foundation, Inc.
41. Jose Ortiz (Jockey) Wikipedia: The Free Encyclopedia. Wikimedia Foundation, Inc.
42. Jose L. Ortiz. America's Best Racing.
43. Irad Ortiz Jr. Wikipedia: The Free Encyclopedia. Wikimedia Foundation, Inc.
44. Irad Ortiz Jr. America's Best Racing.
45. Shaun Bridgmohan. Equibase Com.
46. Shaun Bridgmohan - Jockey-Wikipedia: The Free Encyclopedia. Wikimedia Foundation, Inc.
47. Julien Leparoux. Wikipedia: the Free Encyclopedia. Wikimedia Foundation, Inc.
48. Julien Leparoux. America's Best Racing.
49. Tyler Gaffalione. Wikipedia: The Free Encyclopedia. Wikimedia Foundation, Inc.
50. Tyler. Gaffalione. America's Best Racing.
51. Top Jockeys. Blood Horse December 31, 2018.

CHAPTER 11: HOW TO INTERPRET RACING STATISTICS

1. Details of the Dosage Index, Blood Horse, May 5, 2018.
2. Explanation of Dosage. Bloodstock Research Services, Inc. The Handicapper's Library. Brisnet.com pp 1-4.
3. Beyer, A. Dosage Strike the Gold Bucks with the System. Washington Post, April 30, 1991.
4. Rasmussen, Leo. Dosage and The Kentucky Derby. Horse Racing Nation. February 20, 2014.
5. Beyer, A. Beyer Speed Figures. The Daily Racing Form, 1975.
6. Schmitz, David. Kentucky Derby by the Numbers: Dosage Index. Blood Horse, April 27, 2009.
7. Rogers. Inbreeding and relatedness Coefficients extended 10 Generations. True Nicks, February 4, 2019.

CHAPTER 12: RACE HORSE SELECTIONS

1. Daily Racing Form
2. Brisnet. Com
3, Beyer, Andrew. Beyer speed Figures. The Daily Racing Form, 1975.
4. Beyer Speed Figures. How to Understand Them. Part I of II. Predictem. www.prdictem.com,
5. Simon, Derek. It's time to Call Beyer Speed Figures What They Really Are. U.S. Racing. 2016.
6. Simon. Derek. What Do All Triple Crown winners Have in Common. U.S. Racing, March 14, 2017.
7. Peters, Anne, Sources of Stamina. The Blood Horse. May 30, 2014.

CHAPTER 13: WAGERING, TYPES OF BETS

1. Churchill Downs Incorporated (NASDAQ;CHDN) Offers Year-round Simulcast Wagering at the Historic Track. Churchill Downs Release, 2018.
1. Angst, Frank. A Look at the 2018 Derby Future Wager Value. Blood Horse Daily April 20, 2018.
2. Beyer, Andrew. Beyer Speed Figures. The Daily Racing Form, 1975.
3. Beyer Speed Figures. How to Understand Them, Part I of II. Predictem. www.predictem.com.
4. Simon, Derek. The Speed Nation, September 22. 2010
5. Simon, Derek. Says Use the Speed. U.S. Racing, March 15, 2017.
6. Simon, Derek. "What Do All Triple Crown Winners Have in Common." U.S. Racing, March 14, 2017.
7. Peters, Anne. Sources of Stamina. Blood Horse, May 30, 2014.
8. Steve Haskin's Derby Dozen. The Blood Horse, February 21, 2019.

CHAPTER 14: YOU BE THE JUDGE

1. Beyer, Andrew. The Best Kentucky Derby Winners of All Time. Washington Post, May 2, 2017.
2. Rogers, Caroline. These Are the Most Famous Horses from The Kentucky Derby. Southern Living, 2018.
3. Quick B. The Top 10 Kentucky Derby Winners of All Time. Louisville Life, 2017.

4. Lin, Nina. Run for The Roses: 8 Most Famous Winners of the Kentucky Derby. NBCchicago. com. May 2, 2018.

CHAPTER 15: TRAVEL ARRANGEMENT TO RACE TRACK

1. Maps and Directions. Churchill Downs. Directions: Access from Expressways to Churchill Downs.

CHAPTER 16: ARRIVAL AT TRACK

1. Novelly, T. Heads Up: 2018 Kentucky Derby Attendees: Churchill Downs Has Changed Parking and Gates. Louisville Courier Journal, April 10, 2018.

3. CD Releases Parking Plan for Remainder of Meet. Churchill Downs Press Release, November 20, 2018.

CHAPTER 17: PLACES TO STAY

1. Best Hotels Closest to Churchill Downs. Expedia, 2018.
2. Hotels Near Churchill Downs. www. Hotels. Com.

ABOUT THE AUTHOR

FRANCIS MARION BUSH, DMD, PhD, has written several books including Horse Racing, Anatomy, Physiology, Dentistry and the Civil War.

BY FRANCIS MARION BUSH:

Famous Horsewomen of Virginia
Paul Mellon: Visionary of the Turf
Colonial Downs and More
Dapple's Journey
Richmond's Court End: Forgotten and Fading Past
Temporomandibular Joint and Related Orofacial Disorders
Is It You, I or Just Brain Fog

INDEX

Across the Board 88
Advance Deposit Wagering (ADW) 89
Alan a Dale 13
Affirmed 8, 38, 97, 99, 100
Agile 13
Albarado, Robby 71, 74
Allen, Dud 13
Allowance race 76
Always Dreaming 6, 42
Alysheba 8, 96
Amiel, Jack 10
Amelia Court House 2
America's Most Historic Race Track 3
American Pharaoh 6, 40, 42, 43, 70, 98-100
Armstrong, Noah 13
Angst, Frank 90
Angry Orchard Club 18
Animal Kingdom 6, 40, 43
Antley, Chris 7, 8
A.P. Indy 80
Apollo 14, 49
Apollo Curse 46
Applegate, H. C. 12
Appomattox Campaign 2
Arkansas Derby 42, 93
Arcaro, G. Edward 10, 11, 6
Arais, Juan 9
Aristides 14, 100
Ash Grove Stock Farm 52
Ask Ray 33
Asmussen, Steven, 63, 66
Assault 10, 38, 44, 45, 51
Audible 47, 79, 94
Avila, Gustavo 9
Azra 13, 50

Baden-Baden 14
Baeza, Braulio 9
Baffert, Bob 6, 7, 59, 66, 102
Bailey, Jerry 7, 70, 74, 102
Bakewell, Elizabeth 2

Baldez, Joseph 19
Baldwin, E. J. 60
Ballot 80
Banana Nose, Arcaro 67
Barbaro 7, 39, 42 ,99
Barrera, Lazaro 8, 9, 62
Bashford Manor Stable 50, 53
Ben Ali 14
Behave Yourself 50
Belair Stud 11, 50, 53
Belmont Stakes 52
Ben Brush 13
Best Jockey ESPY Award 70
Bet America 90
Beverley, H. Guy
Beyer, Andrew 86, 97
Beyer Speed Figures 86
Bierman, Cal 11
Big Brown 7, 40, 42
Billings, C.K.G 12
Birdstone 61
Black Gold 12
Black Toney 80
Black Hawk War 2
Block, Benjamin 12
Blood Horse 30
Blood Horse Daily 30
Blue Grass Stakes 42, 93
Blue Larkspur 80
Blumin Affair 70
Boarding Stable 24
Bodemeister 70
Boland, William 10, 101
Bold Ruler 61
Bold d' Oro 94
Bold Forbes 9, 38
Bold Venture 11, 38, 56
Bond, Bernie 63
Boone County, Kentucky 2
Booker, Harold 13
Bookmaker 52
Borel, Calvin 6,7,69, 74
Borel, Charles 12
Bourbon County, Ky

Bourbon War 91
Bourbon Week
Bowie, Maryland 53
Box 88
Bradley, E.R. 11,13, 50, 52, 104
Breeder's Cup Juvenile 91
Breeder's Futurity 91
Breezing – type of workout 85
Bridgmohan, Shaun 72
Brilliant Dosage Profile
Brisnet 30, 31
Broker's Tip 11, 39, 50, 101, 104
Brooklyn Boyz Stable 6
Broomstick 80
Brothers, La bold 14
Brown, Chad C. 63, 66
Brown, Edward 14
Brown, Samuel 13
Brownsville, Texas 56
Buckland Farm 8
Bubbling Over 11, 50
Buchanan 68
Buechel, Ky 53
Budk-den 80
Bull Dog 80
Burgoo King 11, 50
Buttons 13
Buying tickets 17
Byrd, William 14

Cahn, J.C. 13
Cal Expo, California 58
California Chrome 6, 38, 43, 97
Calumet Baking Powder 52
Calumet Farm 9, 11, 51
Candy Ride 89
Cannonade 9
Campo, John 8
Campbell, Frank B 13
Campbell, John 13
Captain Bodgit 57
Carman, Richard
Castellano, Javier 72, 74
Cavalcade 11

California Chrome 6, 38, 43, 99
Calumet Farm 9, 11, 50, 51
Cameron, G. D. 10
Campbell, John 13
Campo, John 8
Candy Ride 90
Cannonade 9, 38, 68
Canonero II, 39
Captain Bodgit 101
Carter, Jimmy 14
Casse, Mark E 64, 66
Cat Thief 70
Cattier Sho 93
Carry Back 9, 40
CashCall, Inc 57
Catrone, Frank 9
Cauthen, Steve 8
Cavalaris, Lou Jr 103
Cavalcade 11, 39
Cavonnier 99, 102
Center of Distribution 78
Central Avenue 106
Champaign Stakes 92
Charismatic 7, 40, 51
Chateaugay 9, 38, 51
Checker Cab Company 55
Chef's Table Buffet 29
Chenery Family 56
Chenery, Christopher T 56
Chenery, Penny 56
Cherry Pie 53
Chicago Stable 13
Chicle 80
Childs, Frank 10
Chinn & Morgan 14
China Horse Club 6
Churchill, Abigail 1
Churchill, Armistead 2
Churchill Downs 1, 4
Churchill Family 3
Churchill, Henry 2
Churchill, John 2
Churchill, Samuel 2
Citation 10, 38, 44, 45, 50, 97, 98

Citation Lounge 28
Claiborne Farm 8
Claiming Race 76
Clark Handicap 3
Clark, Meriwether Jr 1
Clark, Meriwether Sr 1, 2, 3
Clark, William 1
Classic Empire 64
Clay, Thomas 13
Clayton, Alonza 13
Clyde Van Dusen- horse 11, 49
Clyde Van Dusen-trainer 11
Clubhouse, Grandstand 25
Clubhouse Gate 19, 109
Coaltown 97
Coburn, Carolyn 6
Coburn, Steve 6
Coliseum 89
Colored Archer 68
Combs, Don 9
Commander. Cadets, KMI 2
Condre, William J 7
Conway, James R 9
Cordero, Angel Jr 9, 68
Cornacchia, Joseph 7
Corrigan, Edward 13
Corrigan, George 13
Cotton, Joe 14
Cotton, Raleigh 14
Cottrill, William 14
Count Fleet 10, 38, 51, 97, 98
Count Turf 10
Court Vision 64
Court Yard Lounge 28
Cox, Brad H. 65, 66
Cox's Ridge 80
Coyle, Pete 13
Crevalin, Andrew K
Crittenen Drive 106
Crowne Plaza Louisville 113
Cruguet, Jean 9
Curlin 80, 89
Cushing & Orth 13

Da'Tara 61
Daily Double 87
Daily Racing Form 30
D & H Stable 19
Demling, Jody 38
Dancer's Image 51,101, 102
Danzig Moon 64
Darby Dan Farm 9, 51, 56
Darden, & Lo 14
Dark Star 10, 39, 100
Davidson, Jula 2
Day, Pat 8, 71, 74
Day Star 14
Days Inn 110
Decidedly 9, 38, 41, 98
Delahoussaye, Eddie 8
Delp, Grover 8
Deming, Jody 49
Derby Café 17
Derby Room 28
Desert Wine 46
Desormeaux, K. D.7, 69,74
Determine, 39
Diaz, Dennis 8
Distorted Humor 80
Ditech 57
Dominion Republic
Donau 12
Donerail 12, 99
Dosage Index 76, 79
Dosage Profile 77
Doswell, VA 57
Double Eagle Ranch 7
Dream Maker 91
Drysdale, Neil D. 7
Duffy, Paul `4
Duke, William 11
Dulay, Cindy Pierson 6
Durnell, Charlie E. 13
Dust Commander 38
Dutrow, Richard Jr 7
Dwyer, Mike F.13

Eclipse Award for breeders 56

Eclipse Award for trainers 59
Eight Belles 63
El Camino Derby 92
El Peco Ranch 9
Edward, Charles 8
Elliot, Stuart 7.
Elwood 13
Elsworth, Rex 10
Empire Maker 70
Enquirer 80
Enticed 47, 94
Epson Race Course 1
Equibase 30, 31
Erb, Dave 10
Espinosa, Victor 6,7, 70, 74
Exacta 89
Express Bet 90
Exotic wagering 88
Exterminator 12
Ewing, Albert 12

Factors Affecting Derby Wins 34
Factors to Judge Potential Winner 36
Fair Grounds Race Course 52
Fairplay 80
Falsetto 80
Faultless 44
Fayette County, Ky 2
Ferdinand 8, 38
Fighting Finish Derby 60
Firing Line 69
First Landing 57
Firestone, Diana 8
Fisher, Herb 104
First Aid Station 26
Fitzsimmons, James 11, 60
Fizer, W. H. 12
Flameaway 47
Floors - 1-6
Florida Derby 93
Flying Ebony 11
Fonso 14
Food & Drink 24, 28
Foolish Pleasure 9

Ford Stable 9
Forest, Henry 9, 62
Forward Pass 9, 40, 51, 101
Foster, D J. 8
Foster, D.J.
Foster, Stephen C 34
Fountain of Youth 92
Four Points – Sheraton 111
France, Melun 72
Frankel, Robert 63
Franklin, Ronnie 8
Front Runner 92
Fuller, Peter, 103
Funny Cide 7, 38, 41, 43, 49
Furlong 48
Fusaichi Pegasus 7, 40, 43
Fusao – Sekiguchi 7
Future Wagering 90
Flying Ebony 68

Gaffalione, Tyler 73
Gainesway Farm 55
Galbreath, John 56
Gallant Fox 11, 39, 50, 98
Gallahadion 11, 38
Gallant Man 98, 99, 102
Gallant Knight 98
Galt House Hotel 113
Gambolate, Cam 8
Game Winner 89
Gardner, H.P. 11
Garner, Mack 11
Garth, William. 12
Gate Entrance 5
Gate, Paddock 15
Gates - 1, 10, 12, 17, 19, 108
Gate, Infield 109
Gato Del Sol 8, 40
Gaver, John 11
General a Rod 65
General Motors
General Offices 26
Genter, Frances 8
Genuine Risk 8, 49, 99

George Woolf Award 70
Gerst, William 12
Geroux, Florent 73
Giacomo 7, 43
Giant's Causeway 80
Gift Shop 17
Global Campaign 91
Glen Riddle Farm
Go for Gin 7, 39, 44, 45
Goodale, Frank 1
Good Magic 47, 79, 94
Goose, Rosco 12
Gotham Stakes 93
Grandstand 17
Greer, John L 9
Grindstone 7, 40, 41, 101
Graustark 56
Greentree Stable 11, 51
Guerin, Eric 10
Guest Services 27
Gunmetal Gray 95
Gutierrez, Mario 6, 70, 74

H.G.W. Partners 8
Hail to Reason 80
Hall, J.W. 12
Ham, George 12
Hallenbeck, Harry C. 12
Hancock & Peters 8
Handily - type of workout 85
Hanford, Ira 11
Harbor View Farm 8
Hard Spun 63
Hardtack, William 9, 10, 67
Harry's Holiday 65
Haskins, Steve 91
Hayard, Edward 10
Hayes, Thomas P. 10
Hawksworth Farm 8
Head Play 60, 101, 104
Heliopolis 80
Henderson, Erskine 14
Herbert. Robert 12
Hertz, Fannie 10

Hertz, John & Fannie 51, 54
Hialeah Race Course 52
Hidden Schroll 91
Hill Gail 10, 38, 50
Hill Prince 57
Hill Rise 46
Hilton Garden Inn 111, 112
Hindoo 14
Hirsch, Max 11, 61
Hofburg 64
Hold Me Back 64
Holy Bull 91
Holiday Inn 111, 112
Hooper, Fred 10
Hoots, Rosa M. 12
Home 2 Suites 111
Hoop Jr 10, 39
Hopkins, Fred 11
Horse Racing Nation 50
Horse Racing News 30
Horseshoe Racing Hall of Fame 16
Hughes, Hollie 12
Hurd, Babe 14
Hutsell, Tice 14
Hyacinth 93

IEAH Stables 7
Idle Hour Farm 52, 56, 104
I'll Have Another 6, 40, 43, 51, 58
Illinois Derby 43
Instagram 90
Instilled Regards 47
Into Mischief 90
Improbable 90, 91
Inn at St. James 112
Infield Club 26
Infield Gate 110
Infield Structures 19
Invisible Ink 71
Iron Leige 10, 39, 50, 101, 102
Iroquois Stakes 92

James, Basil 11
Janney, Stuart III 6

Japan Stakes 93
Jeff Ruby Stakes 93
Jefferson County, KY 2
Jerome Stakes 92
Jet Pilot 10 ,40, 44, 45
Jim Gaffney 80
Jockey Club Suites 26
Joe Cotton 14
Johnson, Albert 11,12
Johnson, Frederick 12
Johnstown 11, 50
Jolly, LeRoy 8, 9, 63
Jones, B.A. 10, 11, 59
Jones, H. A 10, 59, 62
Jones, J. Larry 63, 66
Jones, Paul 12
Juddmonte Stakes - Boresford - NAAS 93
Juddmonte Stakes - New Market 93
Justify 6, 43, 45, 46, 93

Kauai King 9, 39
Keck, Elizabeth 8
Kelly, Brad 52
Kenton County, KY 2
Kentucky Derby 3
Kentucky Derby Drive 106
Kentucky Derby Museum 5, 16, 17, 26
Kentucky Derby Qualifying System 91
Kentucky Expo Center 113
Kentucky Horse Racing License 29
Kentucky Jockey Club Stakes 92
Kentucky State Court 103
Kentucky State Official Song 34
Kentucky State Racing Commission 103
Kentucky Oaks 3, 106
Kilmer, Willis 12
King, Coretta 103
King, Martin L. 103
Kingman 13
King Ranch 10, 51, 55
Kleberg, Robert 56
Knapp, William 12
Knicks Go 95
Kunze, Eddie 13

Kurtsinger, Charlie 11
Kwiatkowski, Henryk de 52

Labold Brothers 14
La Quinta Inn Motel 113
Latex 48
Laurin, Lucien 9, 62
Lawrin 11
Leary, D. J. 12
Le Comte Stakes 92
Lee, Robert E – General 2
Legislature, Kentucky 3
Lehmann, Robert E. 9
Leigh, R. Eugene 13
Leonatus 14
Leparoux, Julien 72. 74
Letterman 55
Lewis, Bob & Beverly 51, 57
Lewis & Clark Expedition 1
Lewis, George 14
Lewis, Isaac 14
Lewis, Oliver 14
Lewis, Robert B. 7
Lexington, KY 51
Lexington Stakes 93
Lezcano, Jose 71
Lieut. Gibson 13
Lil E. Tee 8, 39
Lin, Nina 100
Lion Heart 70, 98
Long, Charlie 11
Long, George J. 53, 54
Long Range Toddy 95
Longden, John 9, 10
Longfellow 14
Longfield Avenue. 19
Lookout 13
Lookin at Lucky 44
Lord Murphy 14
Los Alamitos Stakes 93
Lotus, John 12
Louisiana Derby 93
Louisville, KY 2
Louisville Courier Journal 49

Louisville Marching Band 34
Louisville New Jockey Club 3, 4
Louisville Trust Bank 54
Lucky Debonair 9, 39
Lukas, D. Wayne 7, 60, 62, 66
Lukas, D. Wayne Collection 16
Luro, Horatio 9, 62
Luxury Trackside Club 18
Lyft Shuttle 114

Mack, Charles 13
Man O' War 80
Macbeth II 13
Madden, John 13
Main Chance Farm 10
Maiden 75
Malibu Moon 47, 80, 94
Manganello, Mike 9
Manuel 13, 53
Majestic Prince 9, 39, 97
Maker, Michael 13, 65, 66
Mare's Nest Farm 55
Markey, Gene 52
Martin, Denise 6
Matz, Michael 7
Mayberry, John P. 13
McAtee, Linus 11
McCabe, John 12
McCaron, Chris 7, 8, 102
McClelland, Byron 13
McCreary, Conn 10
McDaniel, Henry 12, 13
McGaughey, Claude III 62
McGee 80
McGinty, John 14
McGrath, Hal P 14
McLaughlin, James 14
McLaughlin, Kieran 6o
McPeek, Kenneth 64
Meade, Don 104
Meadow Stable 9, 51
Mendelsson 93
Mr. Prospector 80
Meridian 12

Methinks, Warren 19
Middleground 10, 51
Middlesex, VA 2
Miller, Frank P. 55
Miller, McKenzie 8
Millionaire's Row 18, 26
Milky Way Farm 11
Mine that Bird 7, 43, 45, 100
Mint Julep 29
Mitchell, Bert 11
Monarchos 7, 40, 4, 98, 99
Monomoy Girl 65
Mooney, John D 12
Moreno, Henry 10
Morris, Charles Dabney 57
Morris, Greer B 14
Morris, John H 13
Morris & Patton 14
Morvich 12
Motion, H. Graham 6, 63, 66
Mott, William I. 64, 66
Mr. Prospector 80
Mucho Gusto 89
Murphy, Isaac 13, 14, 68
Murphy, Jim 14
My Man Sam 72
My Old Kentucky Home 34, 35
Mucho Gusto 94

Nafzger, Carl 7, 62
NASDQ Stock Exchange 4
Nashua 53, 60, 80
Nasrullah 46, 80
Natalma 46
National Horse Racing Hall of Fame 60, 65
Native Dancer 100, 101
Nearactic 46
Needles 10, 38
Nehru 63
Nichols, T. J. 14
Nike Sentient Jet Service 107
Nippon Nisai Yushu – Tokyo 94
Nobel Indy 94
Nolo Contesto 91

New Orleans, LA 52
North Down, England 1
North State III 80
Northern Dancer 9, 39, 41, 46, 100
Northern Virginia Campaign 2
Notter, Joe 12
Nyquist 6, 40, 42, 51, 58, 99

Off Track Betting Pallor (OTB) 89
Old Frankfort Pike 56
Old Rosebud 12
Olin, John 9
Omaha 11, 39, 50
Omaha Beach 91
Omar Khayam 12, 46
Omni Louisville Motel 112
Orb 6, 42
O'Neill, Douglas 6, 58, 61, 66
Ormsby, Steven 3
Ortiz, Iran Jr 72, 74
Ortiz, Jose 72, 74
Oscar Performance 73
Overbrook Farm 7
Oxley, John 7

Paddock 19
Paddock Gate 5, 108, 109
Paddock Walkway 17
Palmetto Club 52
Panasonic Screen Video 23
Papa John's Cardinal Stadium 113
Parke, Ivan H 10
Partee, W. Cal 8
Patton 92
Paul, Lee 14
Paul Jones 12
Paulick Report 30
Pedigree Rating 84
Pegram, Mike 7
Pensive 10
Pensive 38, 50
Perkins, Soup 13
Peters, Anne 86
Petty, Abe 14

Phenylbutazone (Bute) 103
Phipps Stable 6, 60, 62
Phipps-Wheatley Stable 60
Pick three-six 87
Pickens, Arthur 12
Pincay, Laffite Jr 8
Pink Star 12
Pimlico race course 86
Plaudit 13
Pleasant Colony 39
Pleasant Colony
Pletcher, Todd 6, 60, 61, 66
Pompa, Paul Jr 7
Ponder 10, 38, 50
Post Position 36, 37, 38
Patton 93
Powers, Vincent 12
Practical Joke 63
Prado, Edgar 7
Preakness 46, 62
Price, Jack 9
Price, Katherine 9
Prairie Bayou 70
Prat, Flavien 72, 74
Prime Power 84
Prior, Frank 13
Promises Fulfilled 47
Proper Reality 70
Proud Clarion 9, 39, 41, 51
Proud Citizen 70
Prudery 54

Qatar Prix Racing Post Trophy 93
Quality Inn Motel 111
Quick, Brandon 98
Quip 94

Race Chart 83
Race Horse Selections 83
Rachel Alexandra 45
Ramada Motel 111
Real Quiet 7, 59
Rebel Stakes 92
Reddam, J. Paul 6, 51, 57

Record Description 83
Regret 12,
Reigh Count 11, 51, 55
Remsen Stakes 92
Respell, Jerome B 12
Rialto 55
Ribot 56
Rice, George
Rice, Ted 12
Riley 13
Risen Star 93
Riva Ridge 9, 39, 51
Road to Kentucky Derby Stakes 93
Robert B. Lewis Stakes 91
Roberto 56
Rodegap, John 13
Rodeway Inn 110
Rogers, Caroline 99
Rokeby Stable 8
Romans, Dale 64, 66
Rose, R 13
Roses Lounge 26
Rosario, Joel 6, 71, 74
Ross, J.K.L.12
Rowe, Hames G. Sr 14
Rowe, James Jr 12
Run for The Roses 5
Runny Meade Farm 55

Sackatoga Stable 7
Sam F. Davis Stakes 91
San Felipe Stakes 92
Sande Earl 11, 12
Sanders, William 11
Sanford John 12
Santa Anita Derby 42, 43, 92
Santa Anita Park 70
Santos, Jose 7
Saratoga, New York 64
Sarazen 61
Saudi Arabia Stakes 93
Sayler's Creek, VA 2
Scat Daddy 80
Scharbauer, D. & P. 8

Schilling, Carol Hugh 12
Sea Hero 8, 39
Seaside Retreat 64
Seating, Accessible 27
Seattle Slew 8, 38, 97, 99, 100
Secretariat 9, 39, 41, 51, 97, 99, 100
Secretariat Lounge 28
Sellers, John 9
Sentient Jet Services 107
Serena's Song 57
Servis, John 7
Shaker, Charlie 14
Sham Stakes 91
Shawn, J. Snell 14
Shelby County, KY 2
Shepard, Johnathan 63
Sherman, Art 6
Shoemaker, William 8, 9, 67
Shut Out 11, 38, 51
Signal Man 91
Silver Charm 7, 38, 51, 97, 101
Simulcast 88
Sir Huon 13, 50
Simmons, Willie 13
Simon, Derek 86
Sir Gallahad III 80
Sire Wagering 90
Skye Terrace 26
Smarty Jones 7, 44, 45, 46, 92, 99
Smith, Charles H. 13
Smith, George 12
Smith, Mike 7, 70
Smith, Robert A 11
Smith, Tom 18
Solomini 72
Sometime Farm 7
Southern Living 99
Southern Parkway 106
Southwest Stakes 93
Spectacular Bid 8, 38, 97 - 99
Spend A Buck 8, 39, 41, 97
Spendthrift Farm 55
Spiral Stakes 43
Springboard Mile 92

Spokane 13, 100
SportsLine 49
Stakes Room 28
Starting Gate Rooftop Terrace 29
Stately Victor 65
Stephens, Woodford 8, 9, 62
Stevens, Gary 7, 8, 69, 74
Stewart, Dallas 60
Street Sense 7, 39
Strike the Gold 8, 38, 51
St. Louis, MO 1
Stone Street 12
Stoner Creek Stud Farm. 55
Stout, James 11
Sunday Silence 8, 39, 44, 45, 46, 97
Sunny Blue Farm 10
Sunland Derby 43, 93
Sunny's Halo 8, 39, 46
Superfecta 89
Super 8 Motel 111
Super Saver 6, 38, 45, 46
Sovinski, Victor J 10
Swale 8
Swaps 10, 38, 61, 97
Swartz, Martin 11, 56
Sweep 80
Swigger, Daniel 14
Swim, Bob 14
Sword Dancer 56, 99
Symbols 83

Tabasco Cat 44
Tabor, Michael 7
Tafel, James B. 7
Tagg, Barclay 7
Tampa Bay Derby 93
Tapit 80, 90
Tarai, Fred 13
Taxi Station, Churchill Downs 106
Taylor Bvd. 106
Taylor, Karen L 8
Taylor, Frank M 12
Team Valor Stable 6
Tenfold 83

Tenney, M. A.10
The Mansion 5, 18
The Master 67
The Porter 80
Thompson, Herbert 11, 12, 60
Thoroughbred Corporation 7
Three-Year Old Derby
Thunder Gulch 40,41
Tim Tam 10
Tirol, E. R. 9
Tiznow 80
Tom Broeck 80
Tomy Lee 10, 39, 101
Toy Lee 46
Tote Board 20
Track Condition – Fast, Muddy, Sloppy, Slow 44
Track Kitchen 24, 29
Track Services 26
Trifecta 89
Triple Crown Room 16
True Nicks 30, 32, 81, 82
True Nicks
Troller, Roscoe 13
Tucker, Robert 13
Turf Club 26
Turner, Frank & Juliette 10
Twenty Grand 11, 51, 55
Typhoon II 13
Turcotte, Ron 9
Turner, William H 8
TVG, 90
Twin Spires 4, 25, 90

UAE Derby 94
Uber 111
Unbridled 8, 39
Union Rags 73
Uncle Sigh 72
United State Stakes 92
Upset 54
U. S. Racing News & Handicapping Report 3
Usury, Robert 9

Vagrant 14

Van Meter, Frank B. 13
Vanderbilt, Gertrude 54
Vasquez, Jacinto 9
Velasquez, Jorge 8
Velazquez, John R 6, 71, 74
Valenzuela, Ismael 9
Velenzuela, Patrick 88
Venetian Way 10, 39
Venezie, Mike 70
Vicker's In Trouble 63
Viewing Stand 23
Vineyard Vines Club 18
Vino Rossi 47, 93

Walden, Robert 13
Walker, William 14
War Admiral 11, 38, 97
War Emblem 7, 43
War of Will 91
Ward, John T 7
Weir, Frank 12
West, Jenna 4
Wheel 89
Wheel Chair 27
Whirlaway 11, 50, 97, 98
Whiskery 11, 50
Whiting, Lynn 8
Whitney, Henry P 11, 12, 50, 54
Whitney, John Hay 55
Whittingham, Charles Edward 8, 62
Williams, James T 14
Williamson, Ansel 14
Wilkes, Ian 64, 66
Win Star Farm 6
Win Win Win 91
Windfield Farm 9
Winkfields, Jimmy 13
Winning Colors 8, 39
Winner's Circle 23, 26
Wintergreen 12
Withers Stakes 92
Women's Derby Hats 16
Woodford, J Hal 12
Wood Memorial 42, 43, 93

Woodward, William 60
Wooley, B. Jr 7
Worth 12
Wright, Lucille 52
Wright, Warren D. 11
Wright, Wayne 52
Wright, William 52

X-Treme Transportation 108

Yellow Cab 55, 107
York, Raymond 10
You Be the Judge 96

Zakat, Ahmed 6
Z Humor 64
Zen – Nippon Nisai Yushun 94
Zev 12
Zito, Nick 7,8,61,66

Made in the USA
Coppell, TX
08 April 2025

48066494R00090